SYNTHESIS:
PROCESSING AND COLLABORATION

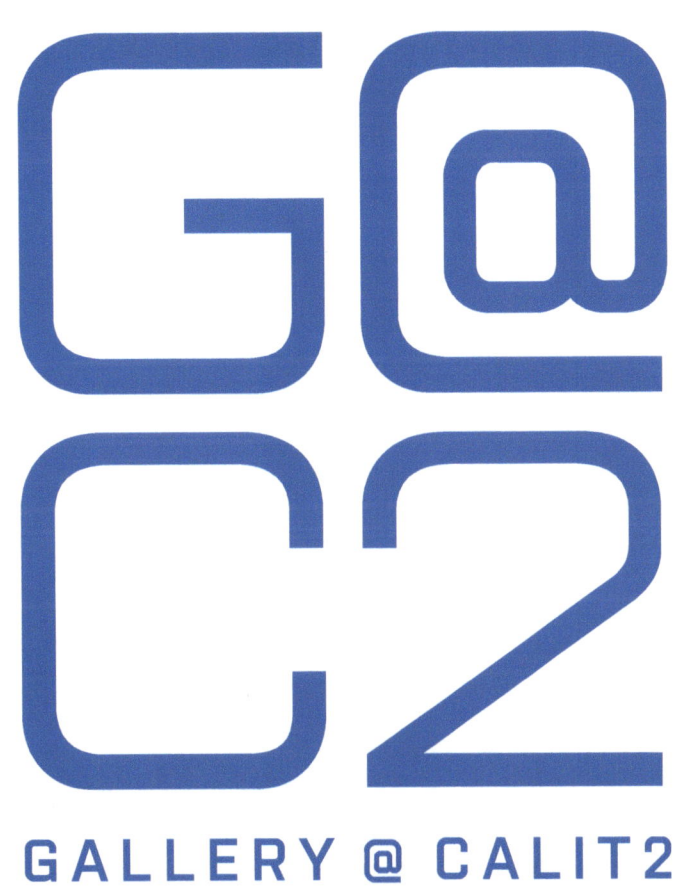

GALLERY @ CALIT2

GALLERY@CALIT2
EXHIBITION CATALOG N°11

SYNTHESIS:
PROCESSING AND
COLLABORATION

EXHIBITION DATES
JANUARY 14, 2011 TO MARCH 11, 2011

UNIVERSITY OF CALIFORNIA, SAN DIEGO
9500 GILMAN DRIVE
LA JOLLA, CA,
92093- 0436

ISBN 978-0-578-07737-6

CONTENTS

INTRODUCTION

BY SHELDON BROWN*

*Sheldon Brown is a Professor of Visual Arts, Director of the Center for Research in Computing and the Arts (CRCA), and Calit2 Artist in Residence at the University of California, San Diego. He is also UCSD Site Director for the NSF-supported Center for Hybrid Multicore Productivity Research (CHMPR). His artwork examines relationships between information and space, manifested as public works of art and installations that combine architectural settings with mediated and computer-controlled elements. Recent major projects include *Scalable City*, an interactive game installation, 3D movie and related artifacts shown at venues including the gallery@calit2, Shanghai MOCA, National Academy of Sciences, Ars Electronica (Austria) and more. Brown has received awards and fellowships from the National Endowment for the Arts, National Science Foundation, Rockefeller Foundation, Seattle Arts Commission and other foundations, corporations and cultural organizations. www.sheldon-brown.net.

I proposed a show of Dan Sandin's work for the gallery@calit2 to recognize the historical importance and continuing contributions of his work to the field of new media arts, while knowing that the challenge of mounting a comprehensive exhibition would take advantage of the capabilities of Calit2 in showcasing projects whose stakes have always involved the radical extension of mediation. Dan immediately put back on the table the role that collaboration plays in this work, and in particular the long-term collaboration with Tom DeFanti, which began at the University of Illinois at Chicago (where Sandin was hired in 1969) and now continues at Calit2. This ongoing engagement of collaboration—in which expertise and authorship are mutable—is just one of several antecedents that Sandin and DeFanti enacted for many of the major ideas that would become tenets for the field of new media arts and media culture at large.

In the 1970's, Dan created the Image Processor (IP), an analog video processing computer. With the Image Processor, Sandin and collaborating filmmakers and musicians created a new dynamic cinema through the real-time transformations of its image. At a time when the image was being deconstructed via semantic cultural analysis, the IP showed a new way to conceive of its material structure. With automated and electronic processes providing novel methods for analyzing video, a new vocabulary for considering the basis of the image became possible. Bit-depth, gamma range, object edges and noise were some of the new compositional elements that analog and digital signal processing made apparent. Over the following decades this new semantics permeated image culture at large, becoming the de facto material basis by which media is produced. The IP was not only used by Sandin

and colleagues, but it was disseminated through a practice of publishing and sharing the underlying circuit diagrams, helping cultivate and influence a broad community of artists/technologists to further its capabilities. Today we see this as prefiguring a type of open source, or shareware, hardware design.

Opening the video image to these types of manipulations allowed for its cinematic expression to become a performative zone. This produced a type of video art which was visually and structurally distinct from both the mass culture of movies and television, and from other art-world categories of filmic and video art of the time. This work had more in common with some threads of avant-garde conversations in art film deriving from poetry and painting than it did with emerging video art growing from conceptual art, performance art and cultural theory. The work of Sandin and collaborators could occasionally be heard characterized as "video wallpaper", but its reach was already influential to other pioneering figures such as Nam June Paik and the Vasulkas. The work expressed an attitude toward video as a stream of imagery which would be coaxed and manipulated around particular occurrences within its flow or act as an ensemble element, moving between foreground and background event. Today these attitudes toward video are quite typical, found in art festivals and nightclubs around the world in the guises of VJ'ing and ambient video. It just took digital computers a few decades to make this type of capability viable en masse.

By the 1990's the Sandin/DeFanti collaboration was pivotal in the creation of virtual-reality platforms. DeFanti and Sandin, along with collaborators such as Carolina Cruz-Neira, created the CAVE Automatic

Virtual Environment (CAVE). Some of the experiences Sandin developed for the CAVE are documentary translations of real-world spaces. In a reversal from his previous work with the IP, where he took the normally photo-realist medium of video and expressed its synthetic plasticity, he now took a format that is entirely synthetic (virtual reality) and used it as a means to create a new type of document of the real world. The experience of this virtual world creates a significant transformation in the relationship of the document to the viewer. The mediation is now providing an experience in which the body is a far more active element than in previous media forms. The image space dynamically reconfigures itself to the gestures of the body and the movements of the head and eyes. The CAVE does this within a space where the body and image have a presence together in the real world. The participation in the virtual space is a performance in real space.

Other VR technologies focused only on the sensory organs themselves. By contrast, the CAVE is a room. Rooms can have several people in them at a time. For now, there is a primary user of this special room, but it is more of a group experience than addressed by other, immersive VR experiences. More recently, Sandin has been developing new types of stereographic displays, despite his own inability to see in 3D. Again, this work is done in collaboration, involving Tom DeFanti, Greg Dawe, Todd Margolis and others. For these newest cinematic extensions (including 4K cinema, as well as multi-screen stereographic displays), he created the film, "4D Julia Set", a visual exploration of the mathematical formula, which itself is another example of how new types of representations confound previous understandings of the boundaries between the synthetic and the real.

Another key legacy of Sandin and DeFanti—these prototypers of future culture—was their creation of the Electronic Visualization Laboratory (EVL) at the University of Illinois at Chicago. This lab was one of the first academic research labs to co-mingle art and electronic technology (the Center for Music Experiment at UCSD, which has since become the Center for Research in Computing and the Arts, is another example that began around the same time). Sandin was brought on to the School of Art and Design at UIC to bring cybernetic ideas into the art curriculum, with a nod to the intellectual legacy of the Bauhaus. Partnering with DeFanti, they were able to pursue an interdisciplinary agenda by funneling their own salaries into the lab infrastructure and operations for several years, building a track record for the virtue of pairing the creation of new artistic content with the development of new media technologies. They built upon what is seemingly a cyclical enthusiasm in academia for the idea of interdisciplinarity. Despite the rhetoric of most institutions, truly innovative interdisciplinary collaboration is often done at their margins. The work that is taken on by definition is not going to fit into existing disciplinary or ideological structures. At EVL it was a necessity to integrate innovation among the arts, technology and sciences. This approach became somewhat understood and pursued more broadly in academia 20 and 30 years later.

For Calit2, their demonstrated success was part of the inspiration for our structuring the "New Media Arts" as one of the founding application layers of the institute. Recognizing that the pursuit of vanguard artistic works would be one of the drivers of rigorous technological innovation, an aspect of the charter of Calit2 was to create an institution in which this approach operates as a guiding principle. Part of the impetus for this show is an account of how we have measured up to those aspirations. From the vantage point of drafting a bit in their wake, I am inspired by the pursuits of Sandin and DeFanti over these decades, and count ourselves fortunate to have them bring this paradigm-generating collaboration to Calit2.

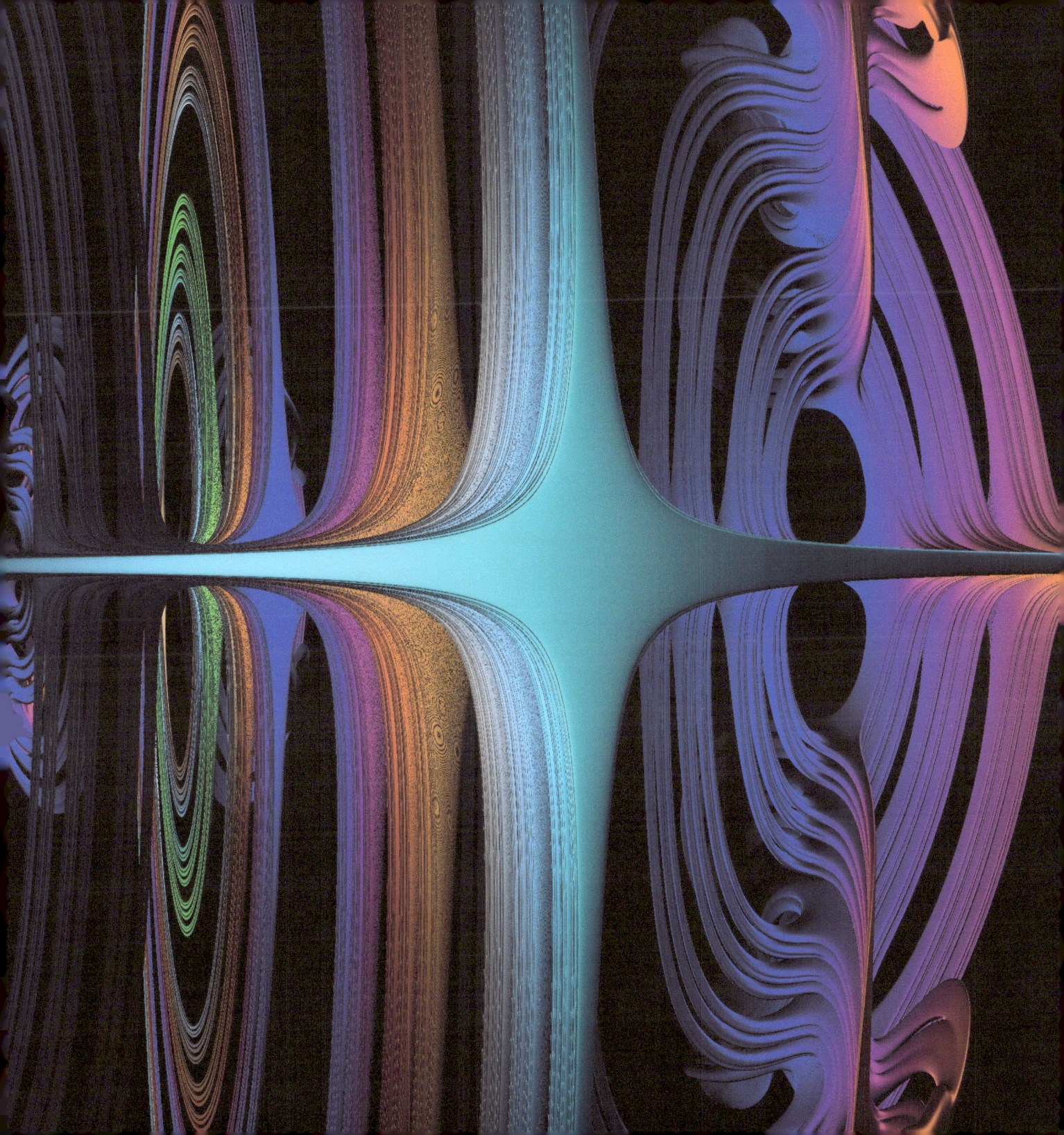

INTERVIEW
WITH DAN SANDIN AND TOM DEFANTI

BY TIFFANY FOX*

*Tiffany Fox is a Public Information Representatives in the UCSD Division of the California Institute for Telecommunications and Information Technology (Calit2).

TIFFANY FOX [TF]: This exhibition features several video and computer graphics technologies that were developed 20 to 30 years ago. Why revisit those technologies today?

Dan Sandin [DS]: I think the intellectual interest in looking at the '70s and '80s video art scene is the fact that in many respects, it's similar to what's going on today with the Internet and the expansion of communication possibilities. In the '70s there was really a communication revolution that happened because of the invention of lightweight video equipment, which allowed individuals and small groups of people to be able to record and create content for the dominant communication medium of the culture. People, as individuals or in small groups, were really not able to use the dominant communications medium in question, which was broadcast television. So there was a real communications revolution that was happening then with the advent of lightweight video equipment that you could afford, combined with the emergence of cable TV, which multiplied the number of channels that were available. In a medium-sized market, you might have three or four channels in the '70s – of course, places like New York and L.A. had more – but in the majority of the markets in the country, you only had at most three TV stations. There really wasn't any venue for specialized information or special-interest information, even in the dominant communication medium of the culture. Cable television expanded that to numbers like 20 and 30, so you could actually have the concept of a channel that the community could have to organize themselves.

TF: What kind of computer graphics existed before you started working together?

Tom DeFanti [TD]: In the '60s and '70s, there were plotter graphics that produced images slowly on paper or microfilm plotters, or the early technology used in digital computer-aided design. There were Tektronix screens where you see a sketch of something, but you couldn't really interact with it without re-drawing it, which took seconds per refresh. At the high level, there were elaborate cathode ray tubes called 'vector displays' made by a few companies, which were very expensive and had huge magnets on them that would deflect a beam to draw patterns made of points and lines (rather than scan in a raster graphic like TV does). Researchers at Utah were drawing directly to TV screens by the mid-'70s but it took another ten years for that technology to start to work fast enough to be used in real time.

TF: Tom, tell me about the Vector General graphics display software you created at Ohio State and then brought to the Electronic Visualization Laboratory at the University of Illinois at Chicago.

TD: The Graphics Symbiosis System (GRASS) was software to control the Vector General, a real-time, mostly analog vector display. GRASS offered script full control over all the Vector General display functions using a host PDP-11 computer. It featured analog inputs: dials, knobs and joysticks. The amazing thing about it at the time was that everything was real-time. You'd put up images, you'd turn a knob and they'd move. You'd shrink them, scale them, add

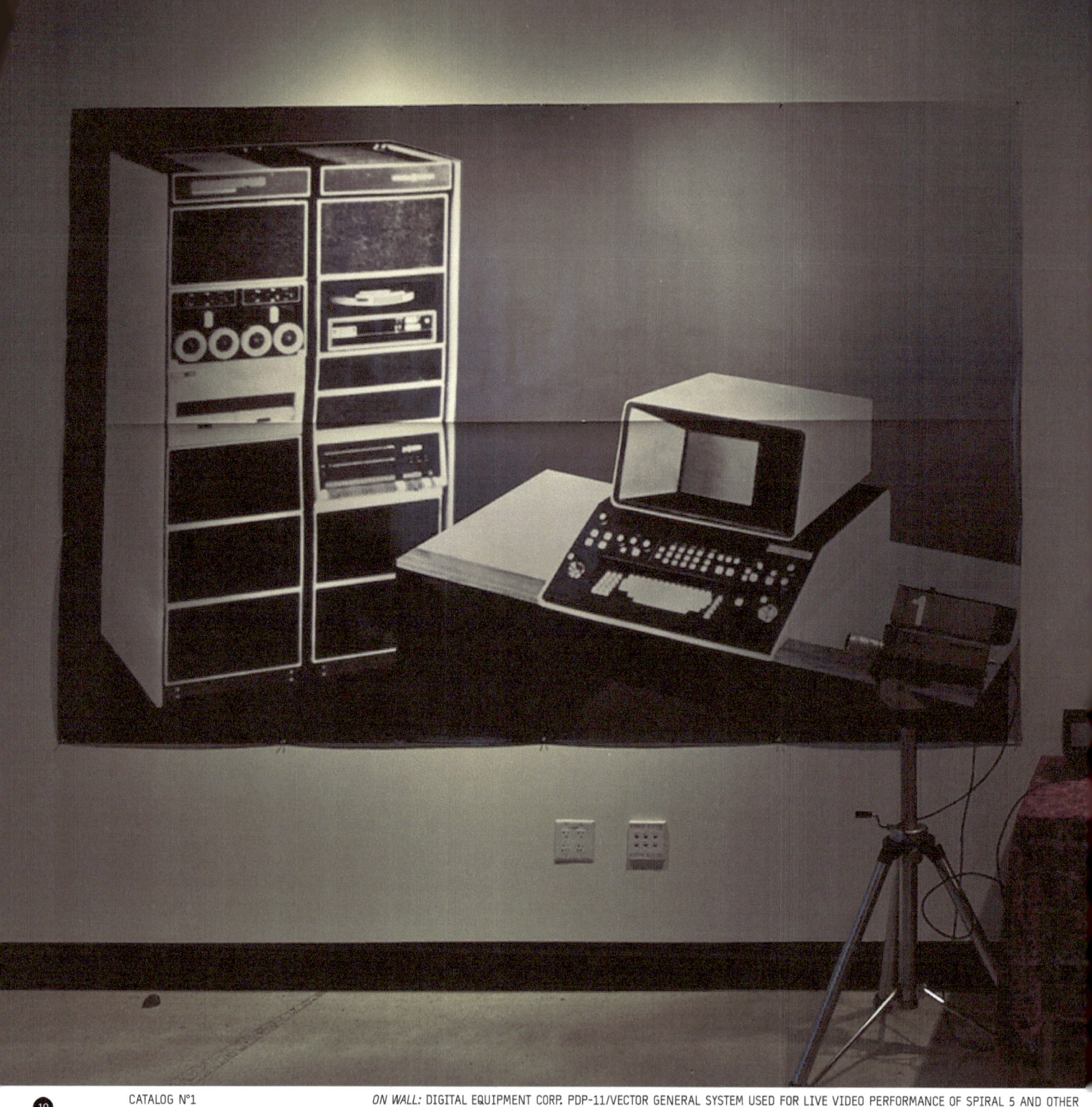

CATALOG N°1
INTERVIEW BY TIFFANY FOX

ON WALL: DIGITAL EQUIPMENT CORP. PDP-11/VECTOR GENERAL SYSTEM USED FOR LIVE VIDEO PERFORMANCE OF SPIRAL 5 AND OTHER WORKS IN SHOW. VIDEO TERMINAL DEPICTED HERE IS A DIFFERENT DESIGN FROM THE PDP-11 MODEL USED IN THE GRASS SYSTEM.

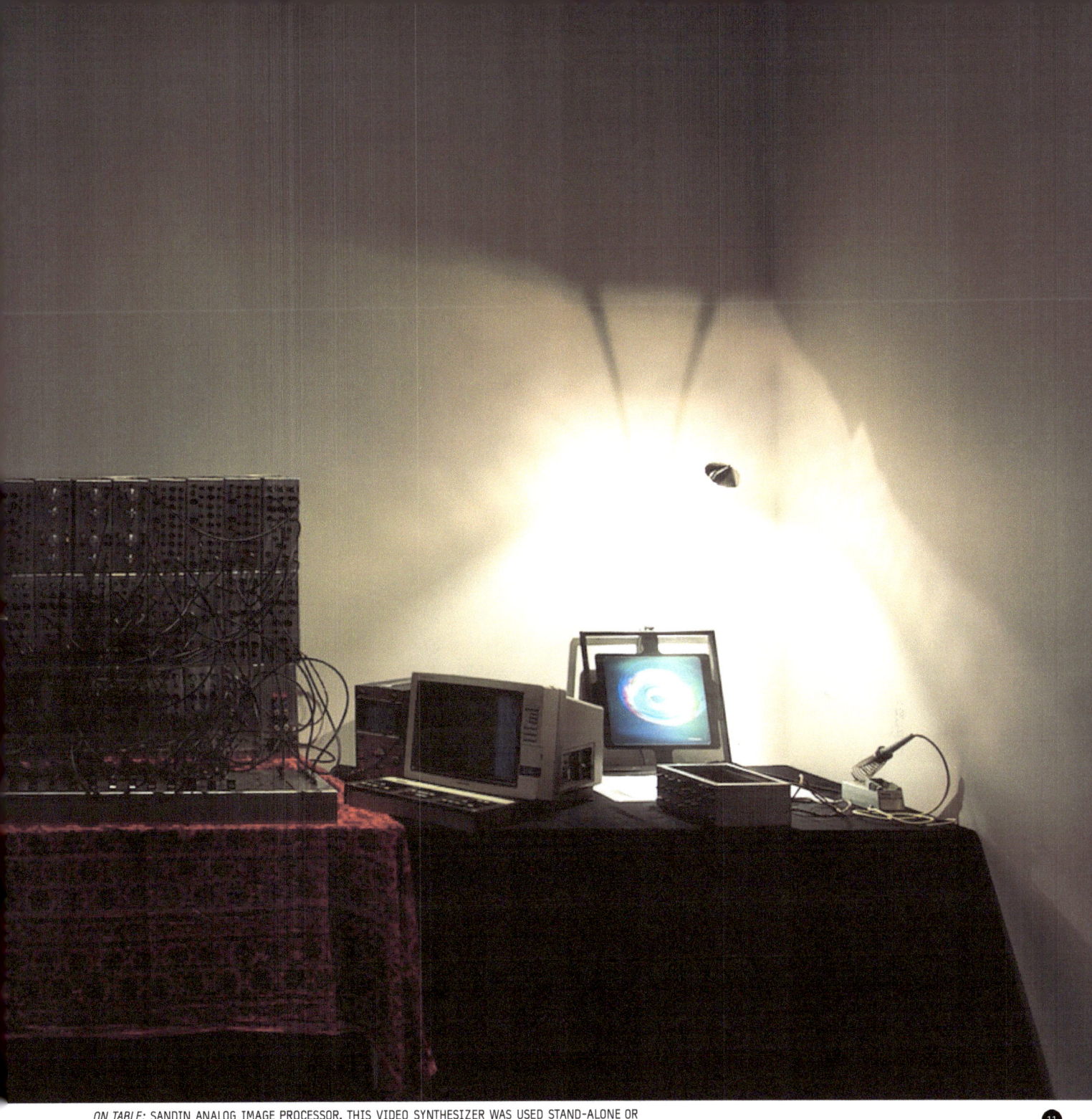

ON TABLE: SANDIN ANALOG IMAGE PROCESSOR. THIS VIDEO SYNTHESIZER WAS USED STAND-ALONE OR
IN CONJUNCTION WITH GRASS SYSTEM FOR MOST VIDEOS IN THE SHOW. PHOTO BY JOHN HANACEK

to or edit the vector lists, literally creating real-time animations that sort of looked like objects created out of fluorescent tubes. GRASS turned the Vector General into a visual instrument (in the sense of a musical instrument) that one could play. Its real-time software constructs became my Ph.D. dissertation. I was graduated, left Ohio State, and was hired at the University of Illinois at Chicago in mid-1973. The program that hired me at UIC was run out of the chemistry department – there was no computer science department in 1973. The chemistry department had bought a Vector General and was generously funded to create educational, self-paced video materials using video live shots and computer-generated graphics, all rather new at the time. The first videotape module I worked on in 1973 with this extraordinary computer system – embarrassingly enough – was "How to Use a Slide Rule." In any event, the Vector General got me to Chicago into a great setup, I met Dan, and I've spent the past three-eighths of a century working with him.

TF: Tom, tell me about when you and Dan first met.

TD: Dan had heard about me coming to UIC as a junior professor and he was really happy because the chemistry department had bought the Vector General/PDP-11, but realized, much to their chagrin, that it didn't come with any software for users. There was no one to run it and get it to its potential. So they hired me and I took it over. I drove up from Columbus to Chicago to meet with people at UIC in the spring of 1973 as part of my transition. At the time, I was very depressed to leave my friends

and the Computer Graphics Research Group I loved at Ohio State, and I didn't know what I was getting into. It was like I was 24 and jumping off a cliff. So I show up, and there's Dan. We both had really long hair then, rode motorcycles every day, loved Marvel Comic books, went camping and hiking year round, were seriously into photography, film and video, and we were both scientists into visuals more than anything else. Dan showed me his piece "In Consecration of New Space," which was the first piece he'd done on the new color version of his Sandin Image Processor. It had a Pink Floyd soundtrack and sensuous flowing visuals; I was just blown away and my depressed state evaporated in minutes. We just got along instantly and started working together,

TF: What were some of your early collaborations?

DS: We have a long history of collaboration that involved a group of people, some of whom eventually came to Calit2. Tom DeFanti and I in 1973 founded a laboratory called Circle Graphics Habitat, which became the Electronic Visualization Laboratory. It was funded by a very advanced vice chancellor of research at UIC, Joe Lipson, who thought we should have a short-order computer media house for generating educational materials for undergraduate classes. Part of the funding provided a faculty position for Tom.

TD: When I was at Ohio State we used a synchronized film camera to make our 16mm movies. At one point I pointed a black-and-white TV camera we borrowed at the Vector General screen to see what would happen. We thought there actually shouldn't be a full image capture – maybe once in a while the TV horizontal scan and the Vector General random scan would intersect and you would see a dot, but that wouldn't be practical at all. Turns out that these old B&W cameras had so much lag in them, and the spot was so bright, that it left a complete latent image on the vidicon tube.

Dan's cameras were these cheap surveillance cameras which also had a lot of lag in them. Occasionally we'd really turn up the lag intentionally to get things to smear all over the place, as part of our repertoire. We also threw dots way out of focus to make the most gorgeous-looking spheres. Nobody else could do computer-generated spheres in real time – and we did it by taking things out of focus. All we had to do to make these two computers communicate was point Dan's cameras at my Vector General screen, run the camera signal through his Image Processor, show the output on a color TV, and record the result on videotape.

I added a lot of time-based control to GRASS so we could automate the knob-turning and write scripts with very sophisticated timing control. *Spiral 5* is the most sophisticated version of that control, in that I wrote programs to assemble scripts that allowed replay and tuning of fluid, but precisely timed transitions triggered by button pushes and movement of dials. We had together constructed an instrument that created visuals in real time, very much in the tradition of musical instruments that create time-varying sound in real time. It was a very tactile system.

TF: Dan, tell me a bit about *Spiral 5*.

DS: Spiral 5 is in the inaugural collection of Video Arts at MOMA [Museum of Modern Art] in New York. It was the fifth of a series of performances of a piece called *Spiral*. It was performed live in front of audiences by people controlling digital computers and playing on the analog image processor, with musicians jamming along. It is an abstract, mathematical form animation based on the linear spiral, in something you might call the visual music tradition.

TF: How did you eventually come to produce Electronic Visualization Events?

TD: Dan's Art Department classes were very project-oriented and typically culminated in public events. Starting with high-school science fairs and college photography exhibitions, I was also into showtime. So it was easy to combine our wanting to do events. The first major event we did together with our students and allied faculty was in 1975, the Interactive Electronic Visualization Event. We used the 3-floor atrium of the Science and Engineering South building at UIC. We extended the video cables down into the atrium, put the Image Processor on the steps with a video projector in a big plastic inflato of Dan's design (one of his specialties). We did another one (EVE2) in 1976 [see the documentary in the show], and then created an edit of works in 1978 for EVE3 which was shown in a 500-seat auditorium downtown that had an early and ultra-expensive GE video projector which filled a huge screen.

TF: Was anyone else doing this type of thing at the time?

TD: Well, besides Phil Morton, Guenther Tetz, and Greg Dawe, who worked with us in Chicago, and the many students, video artist Nam June Paik was a very close colleague of ours who primarily did video art installations (there's one at UCSD in the Stuart Collection). There was also Steina and Woody Vasulka, video artists producing abstract video and a few other people in our immediate circle like Bill Etra in New York. At the first SIGGRAPH conference in 1974, we showed our videotapes on a B&W projector – ugh! – and we then became increasingly involved with designing and improving the video side of the A/V at SIGGRAPH with Phil Morton and Jane Veeder. I became secretary and then chair of SIGGRAPH, which helped. We wanted everyone to come and show their work at SIGGRAPH like we did at EVE3, using the same kind of high-quality projector. In this century, this is all very routine—you see it in every digital movie theater and auditorium Powerpoint presentation, but back then absolutely no one else was doing this quality of video display with computer graphics content—they were all showing content on film.

TF: How did the communications revolution of the '70s compare with the one going on now?

DS: Of course, we thought that this revolution in technology was going to transform the world and allow for a much more democratic and egalitarian situation. That very much parallels the kind of utopian aspirations of people today as taken from the possibilities of the Internet. So what interests me, is that there's a high similarity of the kind of personal religion of people about their connection with technology. This new communications revolution, like the one before it, is being incorporated into people's lives, personal and professional. It's also the case that media artists and students today discover something that could be a communications revolution and think somehow this is the first time it's happened. Although that's appropriate and a beginner's mind is a great way to move forward, as a matter of fact, I just gave a talk that made the claim that whatever you think is new now was actually done in the '60s. I said 'test me' during the lecture, and there's an amazing number

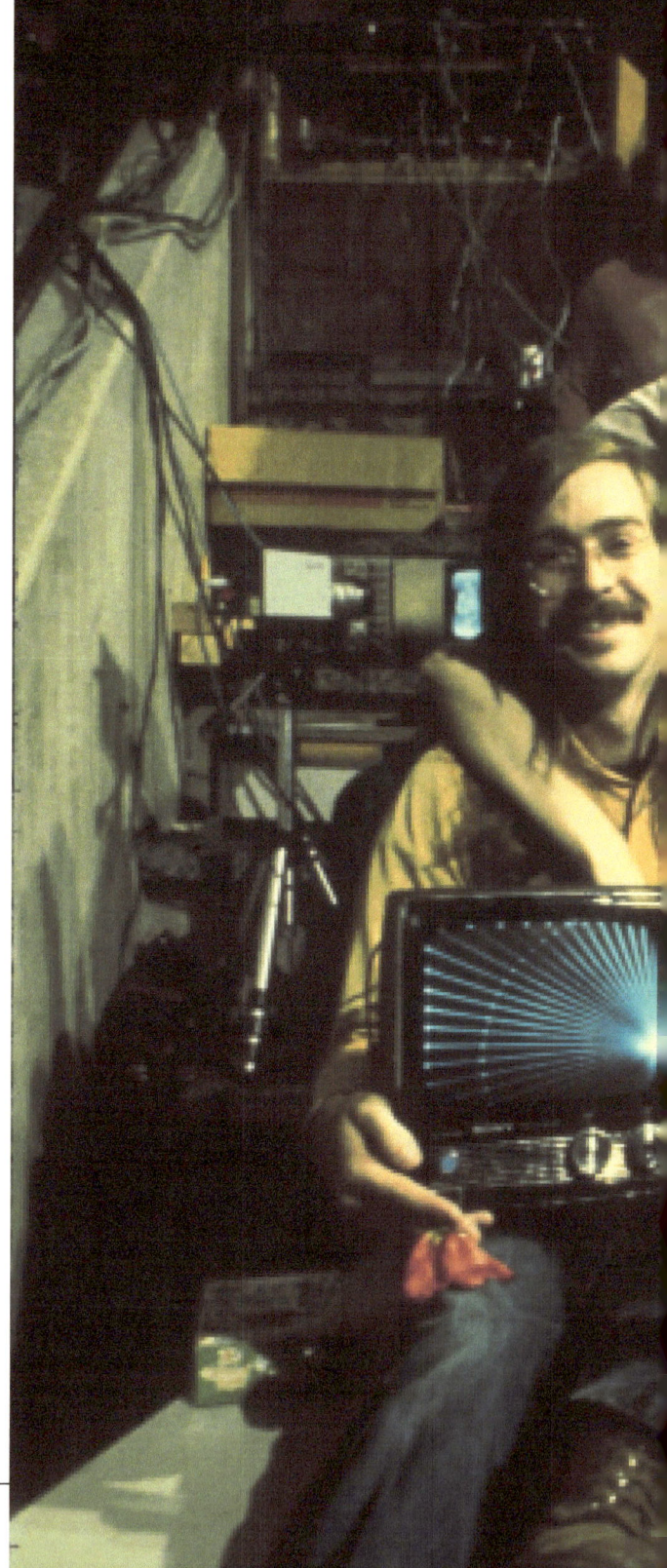

AT RIGHT: PARTICIPANTS IN LIVE COMPUTER VIDEO PERFORMANCE AT ELECTRONIC VISUALIZATION EVENT 2 IN CHICAGO. PHOTO BY CLARK DODSWORTH

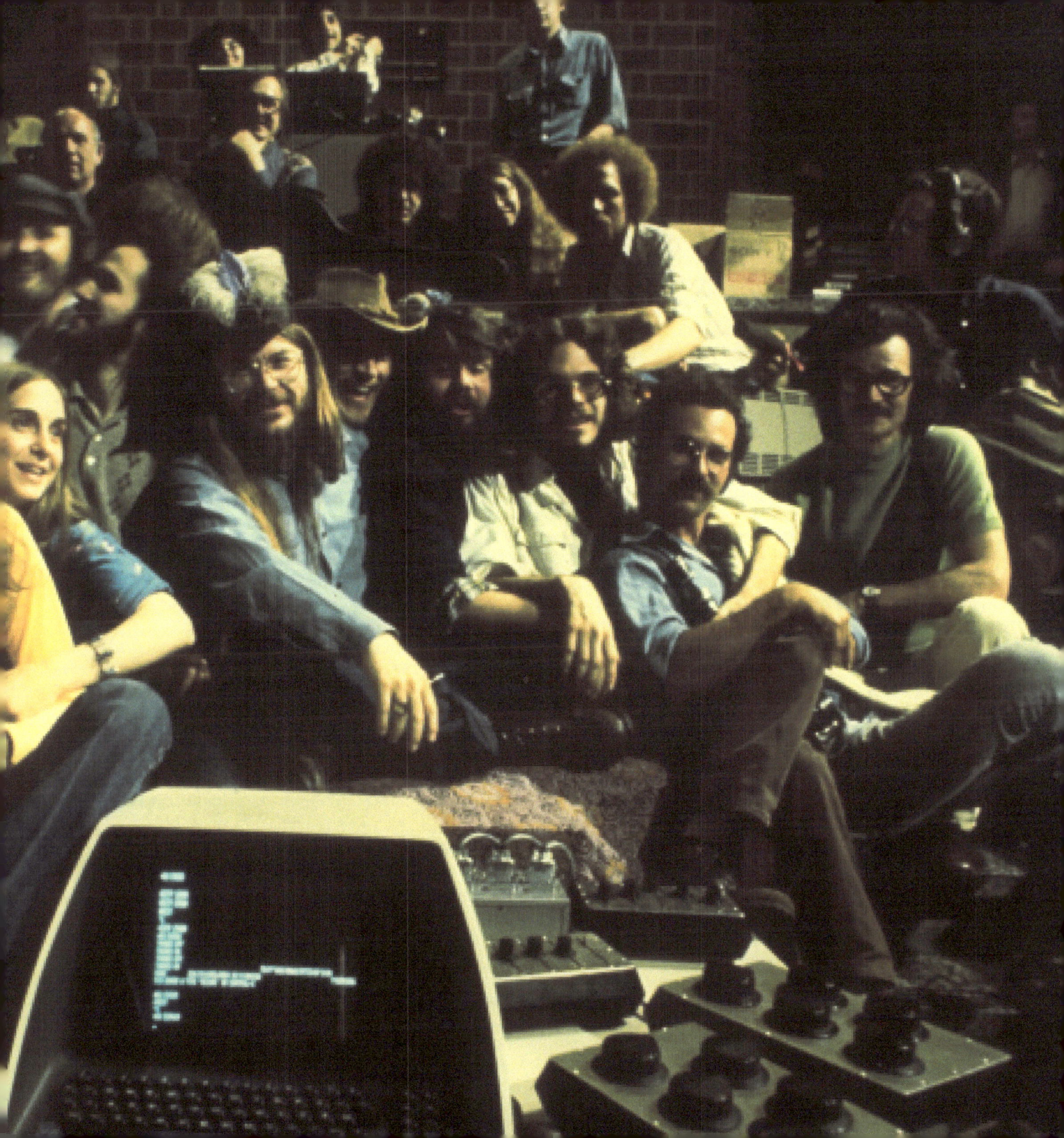

of things people think are brand-new today that actually had antecedents or very similar activities in the '60s.

TF: Talk about your early days working with [now Calit2 Director] Larry Smarr.

DS: Both Tom and I were very interested in filmmaking and photography and expanding our own artistic goals and collaborating with lots of other people who also wanted to use advanced electronics in their art. In 1985 we connected with Larry when he founded the National Center for Supercomputing Applications at the University of Illinois at Urbana-Champaign (UIUC). He understood that although the standard practice of supercomputing was to produce boxes and boxes of printouts, one had to have a much more effective communication medium and a much more effective way to visualize data, and so he involved us to essentially help scientists understand their data and communicate their ideas to other scientists and to the community at large.

TD: So here's this junior astrophysics professor my age at UIUC who, with his colleagues, got $300 million out of the federal government to start up four supercomputer centers. I really figured there was zero chance he would be interested in computer graphics. But in 1986, after Larry had just gotten started, Donna Cox in the Art Department at UIUC called Dan and me and said we had to go down to NCSA to meet Larry Smarr, so Dan and I went down and gave a lecture to the art department about what we were doing at EVL. Larry was there paying attention as he always is – in the first row, us in both high-beams. At the time, one of the things Larry was doing was trying to connect

the supercomputer center to a network – and networks didn't exist back then, outside the military. This proposed connection was 56 Kbits/second, the start of the Internet as something that was usable beyond DARPA. I looked at Larry and said, "So you're going to change the world with a network that operates at 1/10th the speed that my Apple II talks to its floppy disk?" Afterward, he came up to me and said, "You really understand the problem, don't you." And I said, "Well, yeah," because Dan and I had actually done some networking of the Datamax computers we developed over telephone lines, as part of an effort to build home computers in the early '80s and the communication between boxes and to databases was clearly important. Anyway, Larry invited Dan and me to be his first two visiting researchers. So that summer of '86 Dan and I spent a lot of time going back and forth to Urbana, spending quite a bit of time there, and I started re-writing the graphics language to be something we could pass out to other people with Larry's funding. I got some money out of Larry to do an exhibit we called the *Interactive Image*, which was a museum show at the Museum of Science and Industry that opened in 1987. Most importantly, we hired Maxine Brown to come to EVL and work on developing the relationship with Larry. Maxine, Donna, and I took Larry around SIGGRAPH in 1987 and the net effect was that scientific visualization as a serious field got launched. We made EVL the urban ally to NCSA, and, among other things over the next 15 years, built the StarLight network facilities in Chicago to allow the supercomputer centers to connect to their full potential at multiples of 10Gbits/second, 20,000 times faster than the 56K NSFnet. Another important event was the Showcase at SIGGRAPH '92 in Chicago, where the CAVE was first shown in public. Maxine was chair of this 30,000-person conference, and it featured live

---

CATALOG N°11
INTERVIEW BY TIFFANY FOX

FACING PAGE: GALLERY VIEWING AREA FOR PLAYBACK OF RECORDED VIDEO. PHOTO BY JOHN HANACEK

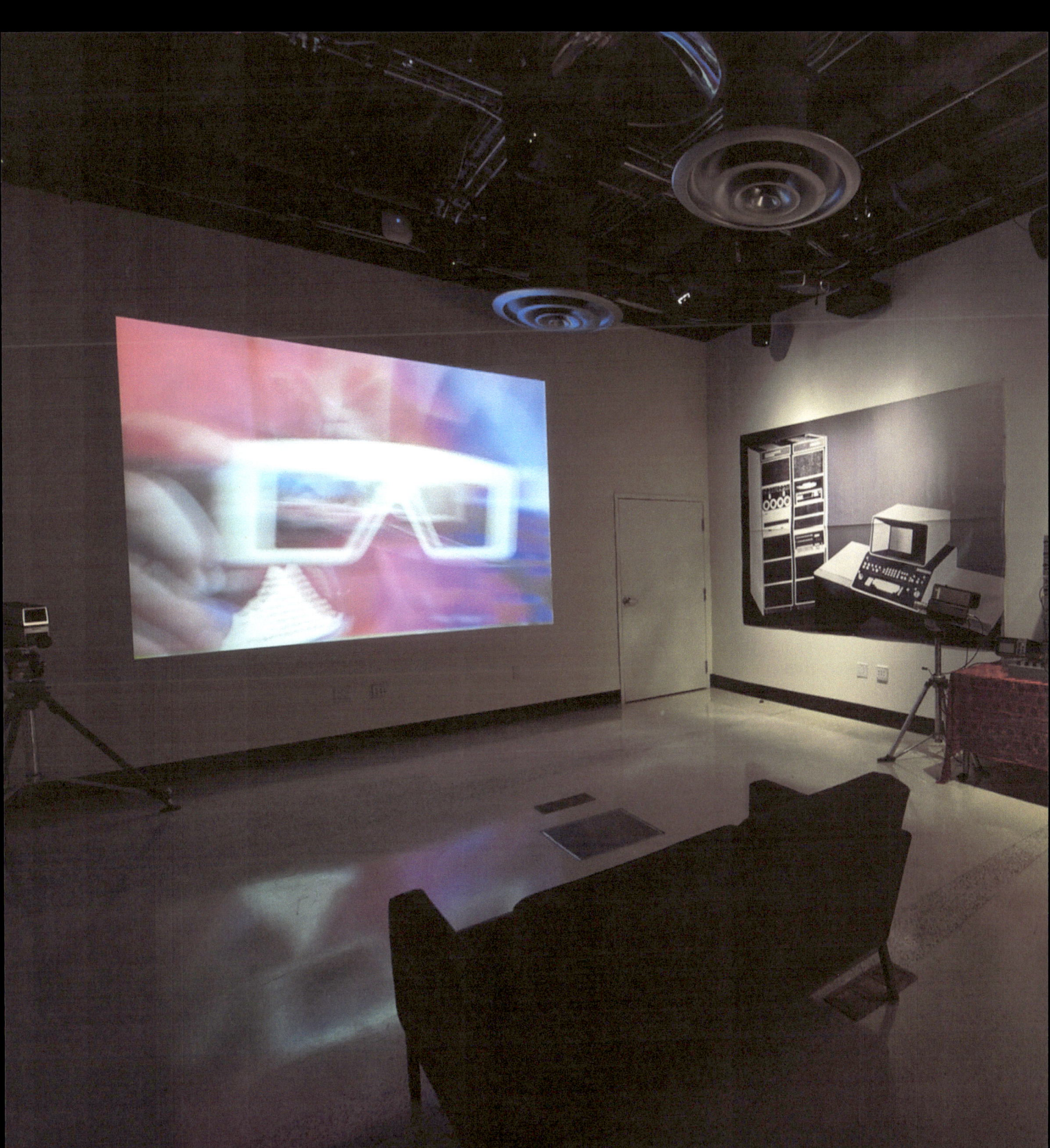

computer graphics hookups to NCSA and the San Diego Supercomputer Center from the show floor over 45Mbit/sec networks. The collected output of Showcase was formed into a 300Mbyte set of science visuals that were incorporated into the first version of NCSA Mosaic and became the essence of the NCSA road show in the Spring of 1993 that motivated the adoption of Mosaic as the visual web browser by federal agencies; the rest is well-known history [with Netscape Navigator growing out of NCSA Mosaic].

DS: When Larry moved to California and formed Calit2, we continued to collaborate with him from our positions at the University of Illinois at Chicago. Eventually Tom moved to California and I became a consultant for Calit2, helping to evolve the virtual-reality systems that people are using here, particularly in terms of hardware, systems software and autostereo, or stereo without glasses. So that's kind of the thread: the people are the same, the goals are the same, the technology keeps evolving and the institutions keep evolving.

TF: How did your own work evolve once you connected with Larry?

TD: Around 1991, we started to have enough money to buy high-end Silicon Graphics gear with the same capability that we have today in game PCs, although it was very expensive back then. UIC built a new engineering building and there was significant building equipment money available, so we were able to afford to get four SGI Crimsons. We then had the graphics power, we just couldn't figure out how to do the screens. Everybody else was doing on-axis perspective, displaying perspective assuming that the viewer is orthogonal to the screen. But if you want to create screens that you're not orthogonal to, you have to go off-axis. Computer graphics systems, by and large, didn't give you the option of doing anything besides on axis, because it didn't occur to anyone to do so. The inspiration was partially the fact that Dan knew how to do the off-axis perspective projections from his autostereo *PSChologram* work with Ellen Sandor. At one point I was getting a suit fitted – and standing in front of the tailor's triple mirror I looked at it and thought, why don't we do that with computer graphics? At that point, all virtual reality was goggles, but we wanted to try to create VR that was on big screens—make a room out of it. We allied with Mike Canfield in Chicago, who loaned us three projectors, and that was the start of the CAVE. Larry came to visit and interacted with the early three-screen version and it just blew his mind. He basically said, "I'll backstop you. Spend all your building money, if you go broke I won't let you fail." So we leaped off the edge and started building the CAVE. NCSA built the second CAVE, Argonne the third, and DARPA the fourth, and then Jason Leigh [at EVL] figured out how to make them talk together over networks, for his dissertation, "CAVERN—the CAVE Research Network."

TF: Why did you eventually move your focus away from building CAVEs?

TD: The visual acuity of a classic CAVE was like having 20/140 vision, where 20/20 is normal. It was very interesting, but it was so fuzzy. Everything else was getting better in computer graphics except the

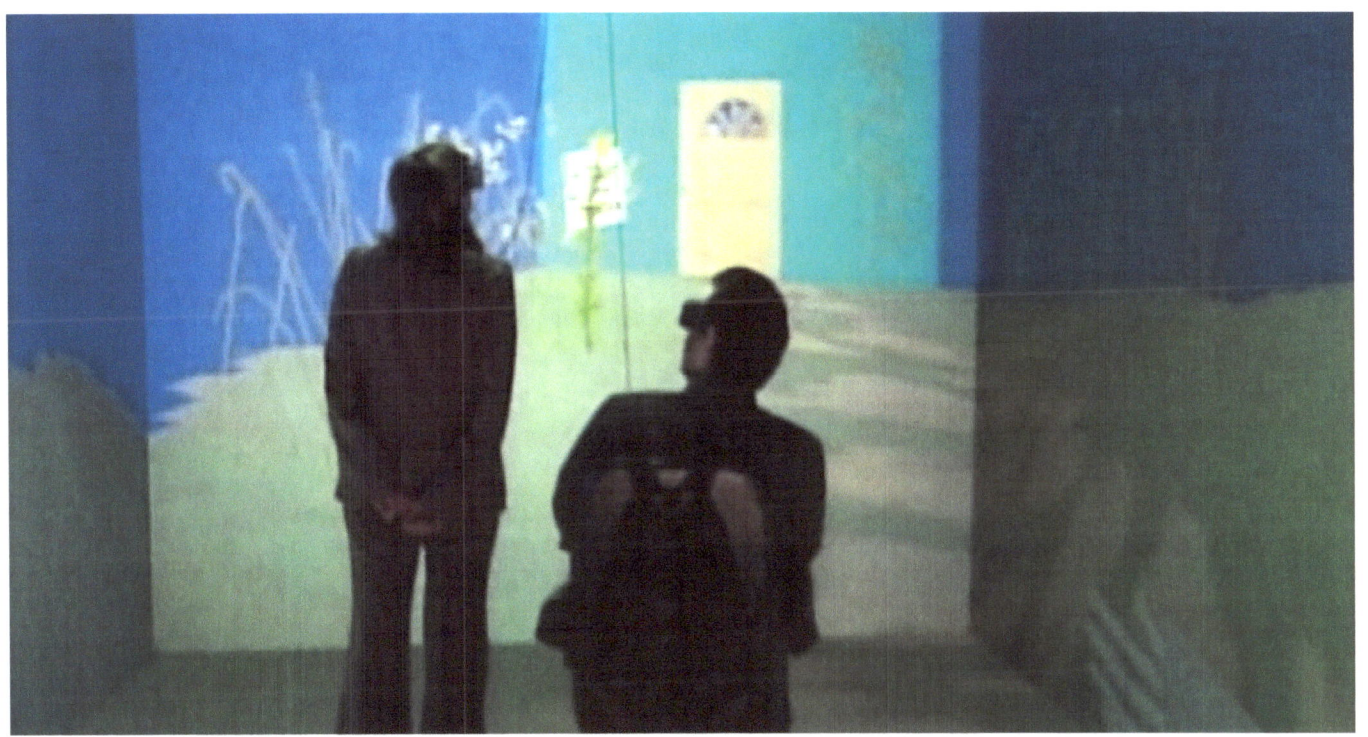

projectors (until 2005, when 4K projectors appeared). Again, everyone thought I was completely crazy, but I decided we should start building arrays of screens to up the effective resolution. The way we were improving everything else was in parallelism, so why not make the screens parallel? So we started building tiled display walls out of desktop LCD monitors, which we later called OptIPortals in the Calit2/EVL NSF-funded OptIPuter project. Then Dan, Todd Margolis, Jingua Ge, Javier Girardo, Tom Peterka, Bob Kooima, and I created a barrier-strip tiled display for EVL and Calit2, called the Varrier, that does 3D surround autostereo—stereo without special glasses. It is still the best depth autostereo system ever developed.

TF: Dan, what can people expect to see at "Synthesis: Processing and Collaboration"?

DS: There is a physical installation of an analog image processor, and next to that are videotapes playing back from a projector. I think people will really enjoy seeing the videotapes. They're beautiful and they're light and they're fun. There is also a virtual-reality interactive piece for the StarCAVE that I've done in collaboration with Bob Kooima and Laurie Spiegel. What I want people to take away is to come and see some really good 'eye candy' and enjoy themselves and get some sense of early explorations in media that will help inform them of what's going on today.

ABOVE: FRAME FROM VIDEO DOCUMENTATION OF THE VR WORK, EVL: ALIVE ON THE GRID.

TF: What is the content of the videotapes you are showing?

DS: We are showing about 22 tapes made by myself, Tom and the community of people that utilized the analog image processor and also the digital computer equipment that was developed by Tom. A significant portion of them are by myself and Tom, but there are also quite a few tapes in the digital music tradition, or perhaps based on that form but abstracted into a kind of moving evolution. There are others that are installations of electronic works and others that are documents of virtual-reality installations.

TF: Are you trying to show an evolution in technology with this exhibition?

DS: There is an evolution there. Much of the same things that interested me when I was making those videotapes still interest me, so yes, there are connections there.

TF: What's your overall feeling as you look back on your work? Is it one of curiosity, nostalgia?

DS: Well, some of these tapes are just extremely beautiful and timeless. Other things are interesting because they involve technology styles of people from a community that existed 30 years ago, and they point to the way people looked and the way people thought.

TF: What will data visualization look like in five or ten years?

DS: I get asked this question a lot, and my normal response to the question is to tell people what I'm doing now, because as a matter of fact, in terms of culture, Calit2 has a leadership role in this area. Of course, there are a bunch of things that will always happen: higher resolution, more color, more compact, lower cost, in the case of stereo, no glasses. So all of those things are the technical improvements one can expect. Beyond that, where scientific visualization is going to be in a few years is what Calit2 is doing right now. It is also the case that my crystal ball is very fuzzy.

TD: As Dan says, the future of visualization is on display here at Calit2, and it's going to be a while before other people adopt the tech, as always. What will Dan and I and our colleagues do next together at Calit2? That's a better question. Stay tuned.

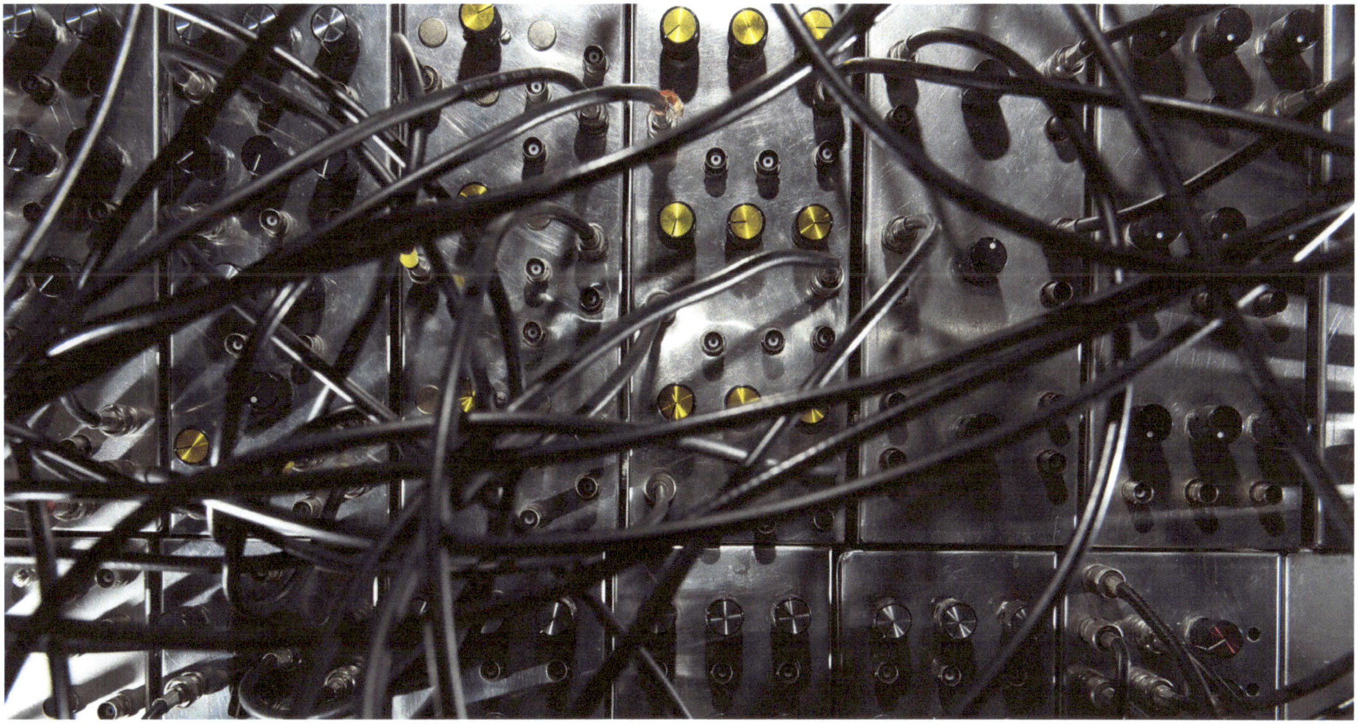

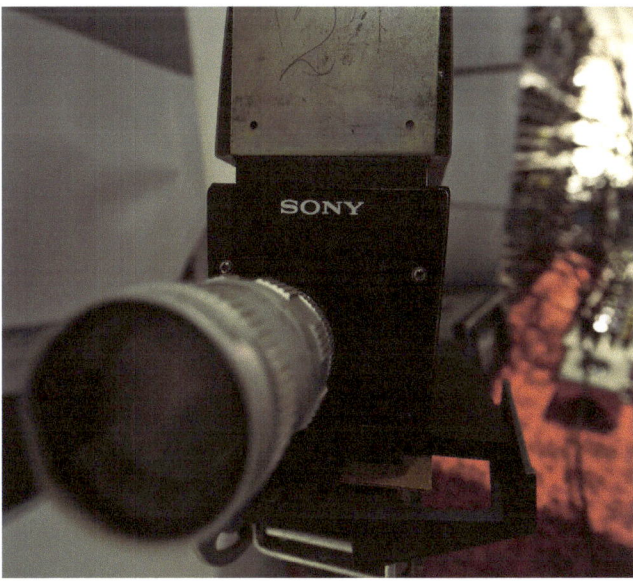

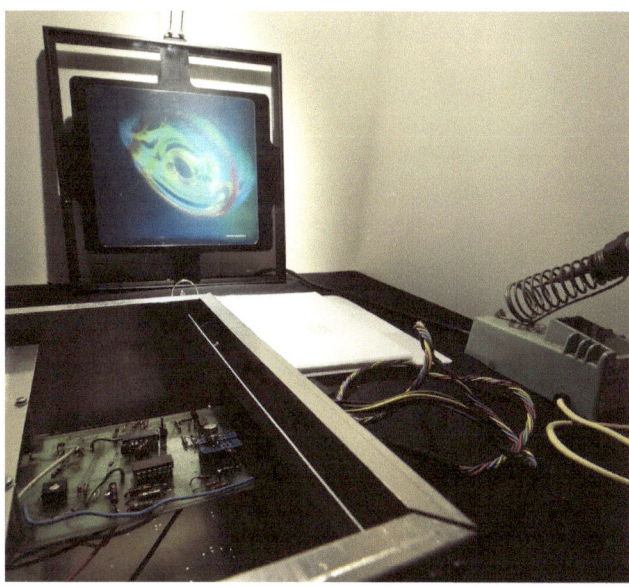

CLOCKWISE FROM TOP: DETAIL OF ANALOG IMAGE PROCESSOR; DETAIL OF IP PROCESSING MODULE WITH COMPUTER-GENERATED HOLOGRAM IN BACKGROUND BY DAN SANDIN; SONY VIDEO CAMERA, CIRCA 1970. PHOTOS BY JOHN HANACEK

ESSAY

FLYING UNDER THE RADAR: REDISCOVERING DAN SANDIN

BY BRUCE JENKINS*

*Bruce Jenkins has been a Professor of Film, Video, New Media and Animation at the School of the Art Institute of Chicago (SAIC) since 2004. He earned his BA in 1974 from New York University, and a Ph.D. from Northwestern University in 1984. Jenkins has curated works at the Harvard Film Archive, Walker Art Center, and Media Study/ Buffalo, among others. He is the editor of several books, including: *On the Camera Arts* and *Consecutive Matters: The Writings of Hollis Frampton; Bordering on Fiction: Chantal Akerman's D'Est;* and a contributor to *2000 BC: The Bruce Conner Story Part II*. Jenkins has been a guest lecturer at Princeton University; SITE Santa Fe; Wexner Center for the Arts; Dallas Art Museum; Blanton Art Museum; Davis Museum of Art; Galician Center for Contemporary Art; Anthology Film Archives; and other institutions. He has written for *Artforum*; *Millennium Film Journal*; *Images*; *October*; and *Cahiers*.

The early history of the cinema is littered with visionary, influential but largely forgotten projects: miscarried inventions (Émilie Reynaud's Praxinoscope, destroyed by its distraught maker); failed ventures (the cumbersome Bioscop by the Skladanowsky brothers from Berlin); and even ominous disappearances (the Frenchman Augustin Le Prince at work in England, who vanished along with his patent application for a camera that used paper-roll film). The successful inventors—Edison in America, the Lumière brothers in France—were the ones with a ready infrastructure of material resources, equipment and personnel. Inventiveness, it turns out, is not enough.

While far more recent, the medium of video, too, has had its share of pioneering cul-de-sacs and lost works, ranging from Nam June Paik's "Wobbulator" and Shirley Clarke's Tee Pee Videospace Troupe to Andy Warhol's unplayable series of tapes made on Norelco's slant-scan video recorder. Included in this select company I would place the live video jams known as EVE (Electronic Video Events) that were staged episodically beginning in 1975 in Chicago. Featuring "artist-technologist" Dan Sandin, graphics software designer Tom DeFanti, video maker Phil Morton, sound artist Bob Snyder as well as a shifting cast of visiting artists and students, these were resolutely live performances in which video was deployed, as media historian Gene Youngblood has noted, "as a tool for the production of commodities (programs, artworks) and . . . an instrument of personal transformation."[1] While Sandin's Image Processor (IP), a key component of these events, did enter into the history of the medium, these influential multimedia programs have remained hiding in plain sight for more than three decades, as has much of the pioneering work of Dan Sandin.

Trained as a physicist, the Illinois-born Sandin had already begun making his own Super-8mm films and collaborating on light shows prior to his involvement with video. A major influence was the celebrated avant-garde film OFFON (1967), by West Coast artist Scott Bartlett, a pioneering work in a form that Youngblood called "videographic cinema."[2] At the time Sandin was completing his graduate degree at the University of Wisconsin and actively involved in color photography, working on slides and visual transparencies for light shows, and even venturing into kinetic installation. Bartlett's film, which mixed optical printing with video effects—what the filmmaker presciently described as "crossbreeding information"[3]—vividly demonstrated the new medium's potential for visual abstraction. For Sandin it represented the leading edge of the visual music movement pioneered by John and James Whitney a decade and a half earlier and suggested a new production method: "I was involved in using optical and chemical processes to create images that I found interesting, and it occurred to me that I could do it electronically."[4]

Equally significant for Sandin was his first hands-on experience with video, which came in 1970 during the student unrest following the U.S. invasion of Cambodia and the shootings at Kent State. By this time he had relocated to the University of Illinois at Chicago (UIC) to work on integrating computers into the arts curriculum. When the campus shut down in the face of student protests, the art department remained open. Sandin was able to deploy the school's cache of video equipment to serve as information kiosks for daily rallies and meetings as well as to service overflow crowds with live, closed-circuit feeds of speeches and discussions. As Sandin recalled, "There was something about the black-and-white image that I found very attractive and tactile." This encounter with video, combined with the hybrid forms that he called "false color still photography" and "stillies" (essentially, video grabs of the water rippling on Lake Michigan)[5], would lead Sandin to develop his own image-processing technology.

The device itself was modeled on the Moog 2 audio synthesizer, a patch-programmable instrument with which Sandin had become acquainted in his experience with light shows. Like the Moog, the video synthesizer would be capable of processing an array of electronic input in real time, and additionally transform live feeds into abstract imagery. While the idea was entirely developed, the construction of the device—essentially an analog computer optimized for processing television signals—would consume nearly three years, requiring this nuclear physicist to relearn the fundamentals of circuit design and assembly. The finished instrument was a modular device arrayed most often on a tabletop and consisting of ten discrete analog modules connected to a sync generator and encoder. As Christine Tamblyn has noted, the Image Processor "emulates photographic darkroom techniques: colorization, solarization, superimposition, burning and dodging" as well as "many electronic functions for which there are no darkroom counterparts."[6]

In what would become perhaps Dan Sandin's most widely shown work, *Five Minute Romp Through the IP* (1973), the artist-technologist—wearing something resembling an ancient Viking helmet—demonstrates the inner workings of the apparatus module by module, emphasizing the simplicity of control, while illustrating the myriad possibilities it held for combining visual effects. Taped in the winter (registered by a brief image of snow falling outside an adjacent window), the video shows Sandin working in real time to transform the closed-circuit feed of the image, which is documenting the demonstration, by turning knobs, moving slider controls, and rerouting cables. Starting with simple black-and-white effects, he patches the live camera signal into the comparator module and then adjusts a knob on the output module to transform the image into something resembling a high-contrast photographic Kodalith, which in turn can be varied along the gray scale. More complex effects are shown by ganging together several of the modules, and then, near the end of the tape, there is a 'eureka' moment as the color modules that Sandin had completed in the summer are unveiled. As striking as some of the prior imagery was, we enter a very different realm with the addition of color, which connects directly to the spectral shifts and cyber-psychedelic imagery of Bartlett's film. Countering the mildly hallucinatory quality of the color abstraction, the tape ends on a humorous note as the artist—in hues of acid lime and ultramarine blue—turns toward the camera and queries the viewer, "Complex enough?"

As the tape made abundantly clear, Sandin had attained his goal of building a device with a real-time capacity to process imagery. This capability led to other applications that went beyond the IP's role as a post-production tool, and, as Lucinda Furlong has noted, it soon became "a performance instrument" that could be "patched together with an audio synthesizer and 'played.'"[7] In April 1975, the first Interactive Electronic Visualization Event was presented as a live performance on the UIC campus. Shortened to the acronym v, which eloquently captured the sense of both the genesis of a new medium and an Edenic arena for artistic exploration, the program concluded with the premiere of a new multimedia piece titled *Spiral*. This work placed the IP in the center of an electronic audio-visual jam in which images generated by his UIC colleague Tom DeFanti's computer-graphics system were played through and processed live by the IP in tandem with an electronic score performed by the sound artist Bob Snyder. Reminiscent of the metamorphic visual forms, perceptual play and spiritual exploration encountered in the films of the Whitney brothers, *Spiral* equally embraced the dynamics of real-time processing and trans-medial improvisation. Like a jazz performance, EVE provided the context for a unique work of art to be produced by a group of artists and experienced by an audience simultaneously.

The collective, communal nature of the EVE performances was as significant as the emphasis on image processing; it became the hallmark of a "Chicago School" of video art. The IP had been developed with an Illinois

AT RIGHT: INFLATABLE TV SET INSTALLATION WITH SEARS TOWER IN BACKGROUND; VIDEOTAPE PLAYBACK ON PROJECTION SCREEN IN CRABAPPLE TREE GARDEN AT UNIVERSITY OF ILLINOIS AT CHICAGO. PHOTO BY KEN REHOR

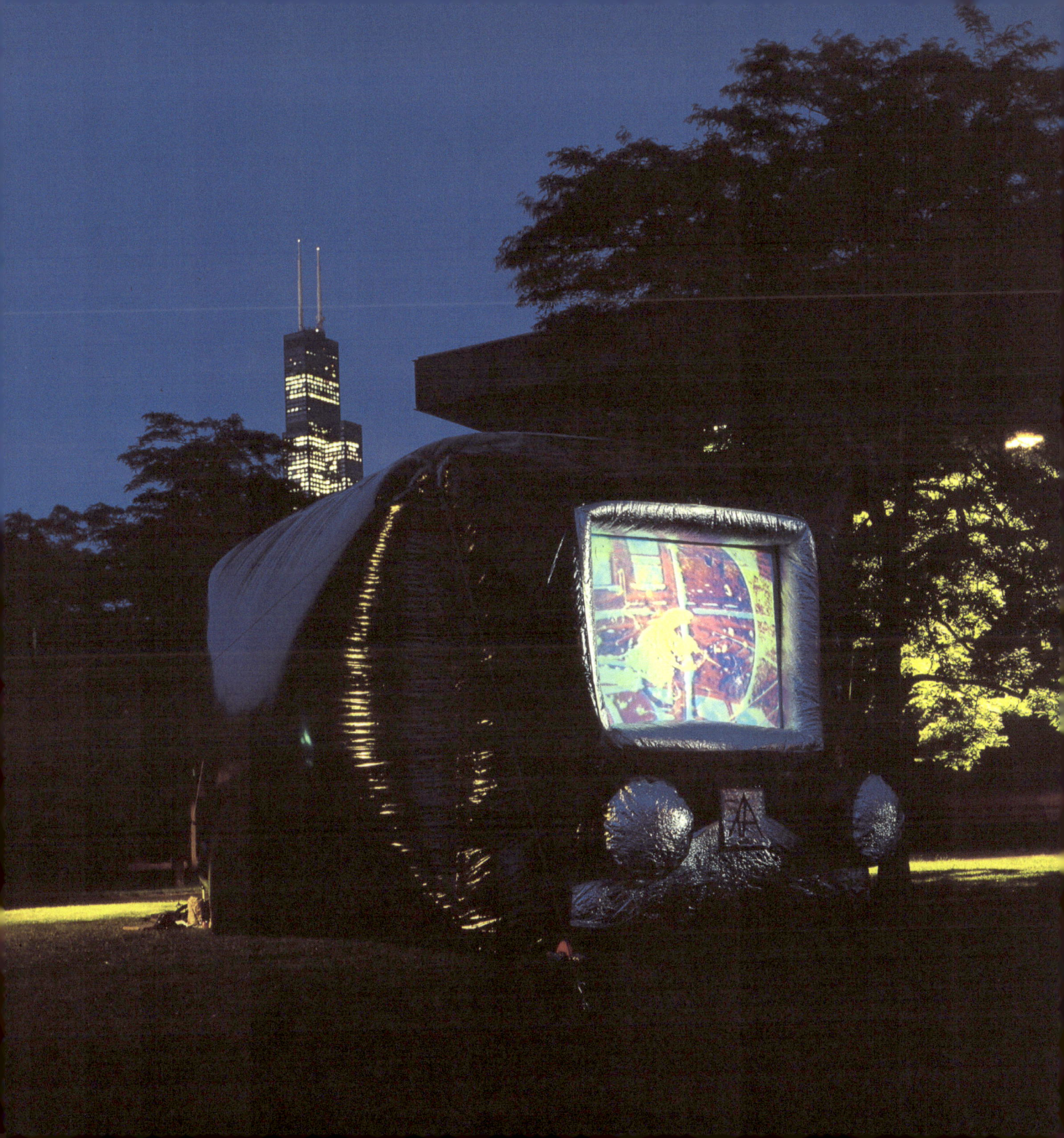

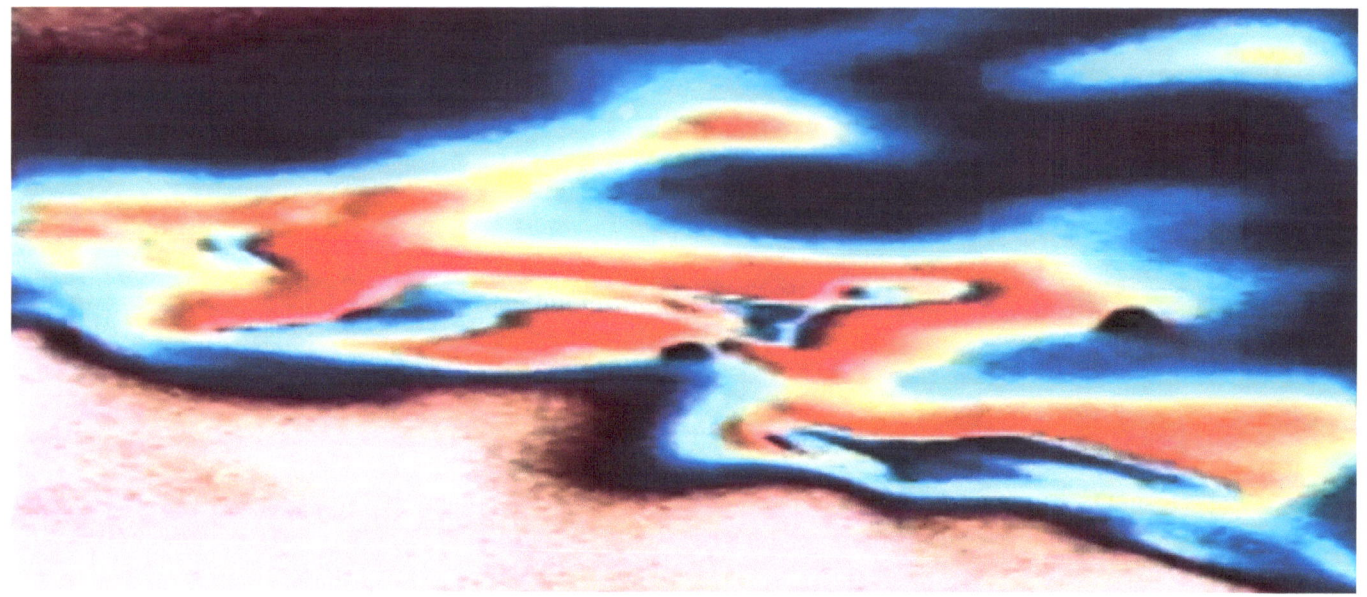

Arts Council grant, and Sandin himself was working full-time at a state university, where his position involved working creatively with computer technology. One of his goals in constructing the IP was to create an affordable tool for artists and students, rather than a device for the commercial market. As Sandin has noted, "In the forefront of my mind when designing the AIP [the first, analog version of the IP] was its use as an educational instrument (learning machine)."[8] So when he was approached by Phil Morton, who had started a pioneering video program at the School of the Art Institute of Chicago, about obtaining an IP for his work, Sandin made a simple decision with enormous implications for the field. "The Image Processor may be copied by individuals and not-for-profit institutions without charge."[9] In making the plans for his device available to anyone who requested them, Sandin confirmed the dominance of a DIY aesthetic within his community, while taking a position that anticipated the broad-based emergence of shareware and open-source programming in the digital era.

Together with Morton, Sandin began documenting his invention. The ensuing dossier, which they titled *Distribution Religion*, comprised more than a hundred pages crammed with parts lists, descriptions and definitions, wiring diagrams, as well as practical advice and tips. For the cost of postage anyone could have the plans, and over the next several years some two dozen or so Sandin Image Processors were built. Sandin began work on a digital version of the IP, taking the lessons learned from his experience building and "playing" the instrument into both performances and the production of single-channel tapes. While as Tamblyn has noted, his videotapes "functioned primarily as ongoing research reports,"[10] his work retained a strong connection to its roots in visual music. Sandin's *Wandawega Waters* (1979) was one of the first works created with the digital image colorizer (the DIC), a digital module that was part of the analog IP and a test for ideas Sandin would use in the design of a standalone DIP. The DIC transformed imagery taken over the course of a day and

ABOVE: FRAME FROM VIDEOTAPE OF WANDAWEGA WATERS.

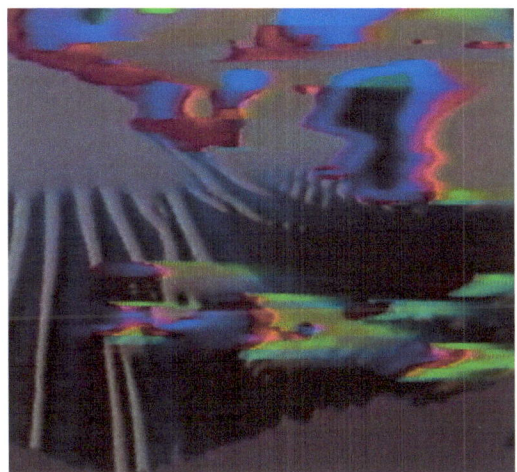

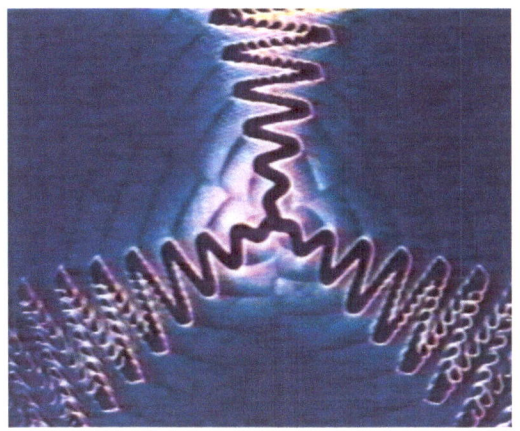

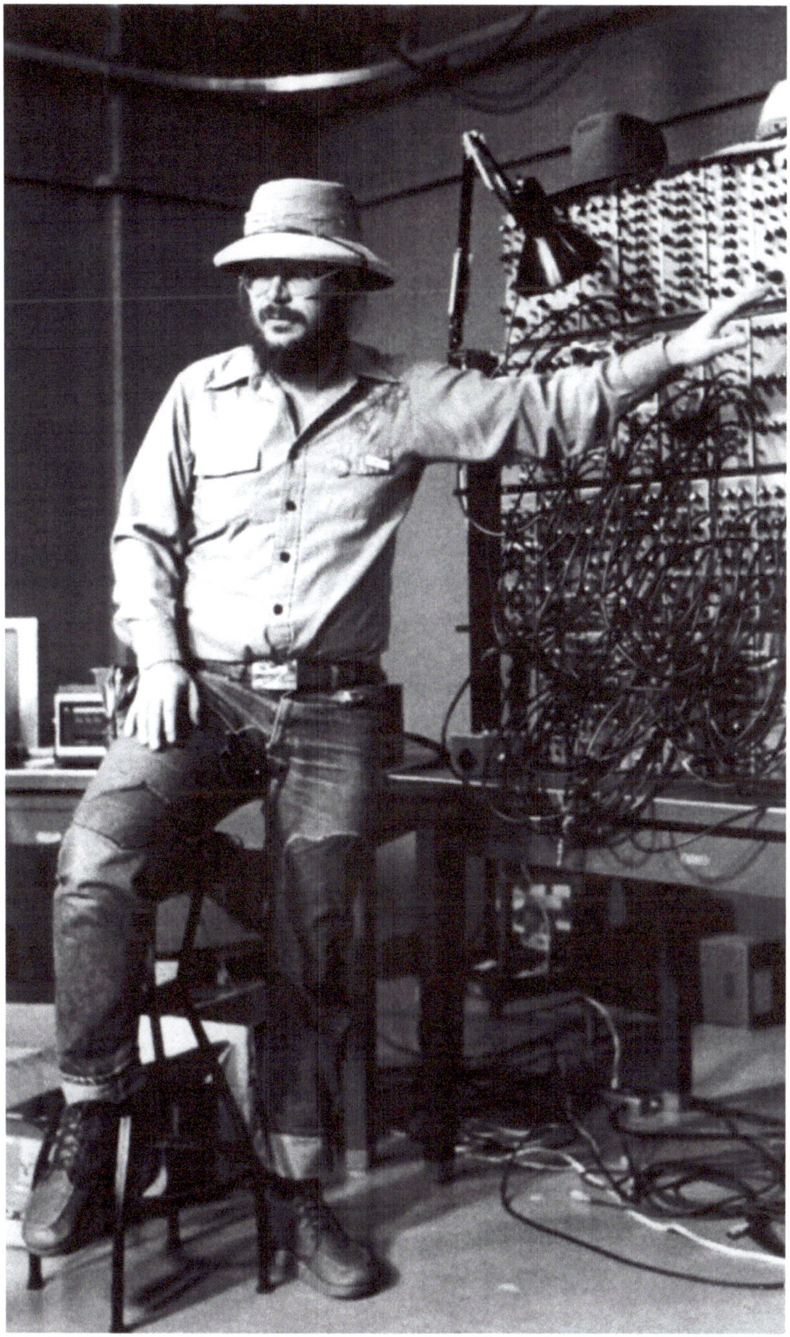

CLOCKWISE FROM TOP LEFT: FRAME FROM VIDEOTAPE, *COLORFULL COLORADO* [SIC]; DAN SANDIN IN FRONT OF PHIL MORTON'S COPY OF THE IMAGE PROCESSOR; AND FRAME FROM VIDEOTAPE OF *SPIRAL 5*.

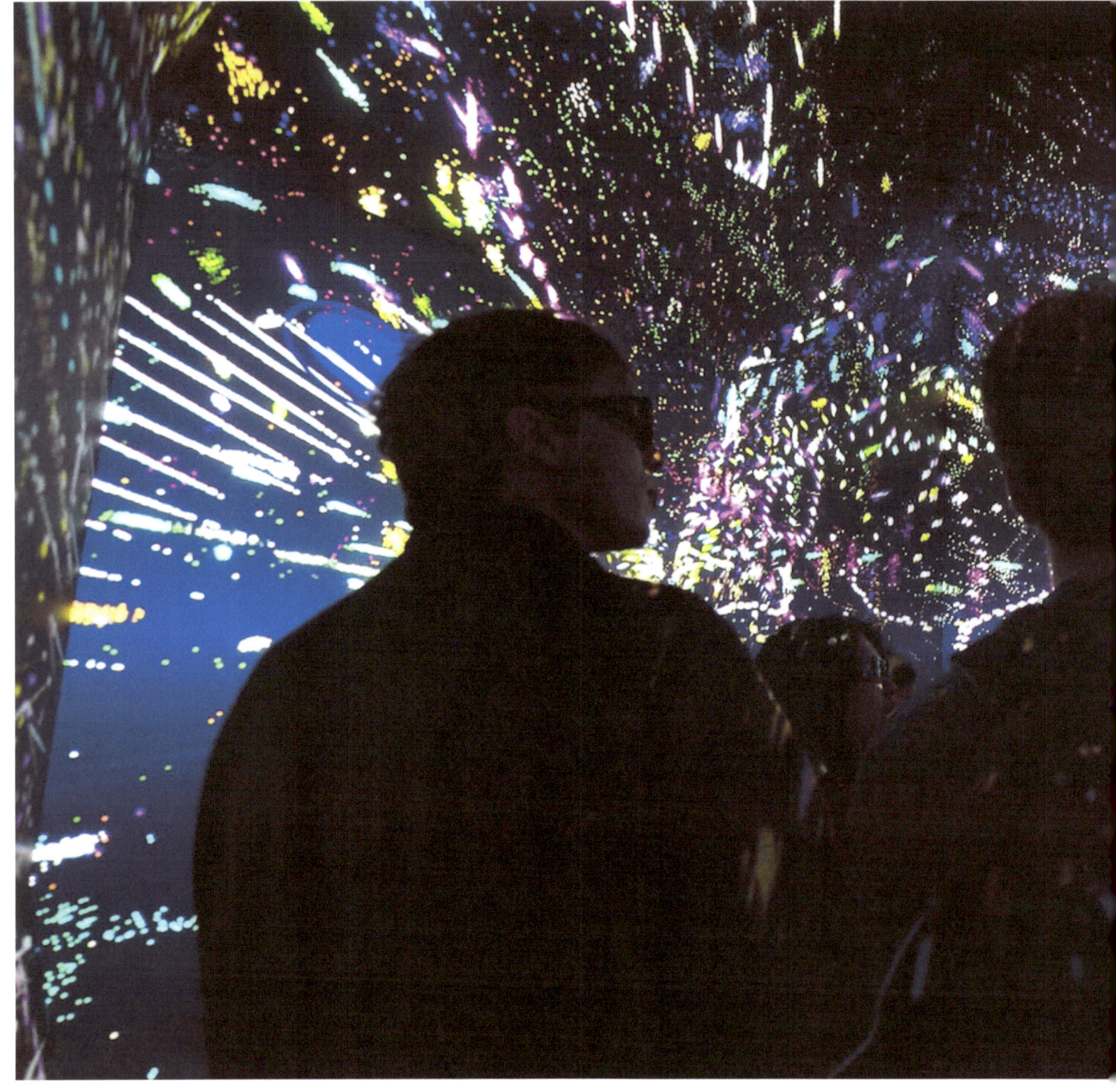

CATALOG N°11
ESSAY BY BRUCE JENKINS

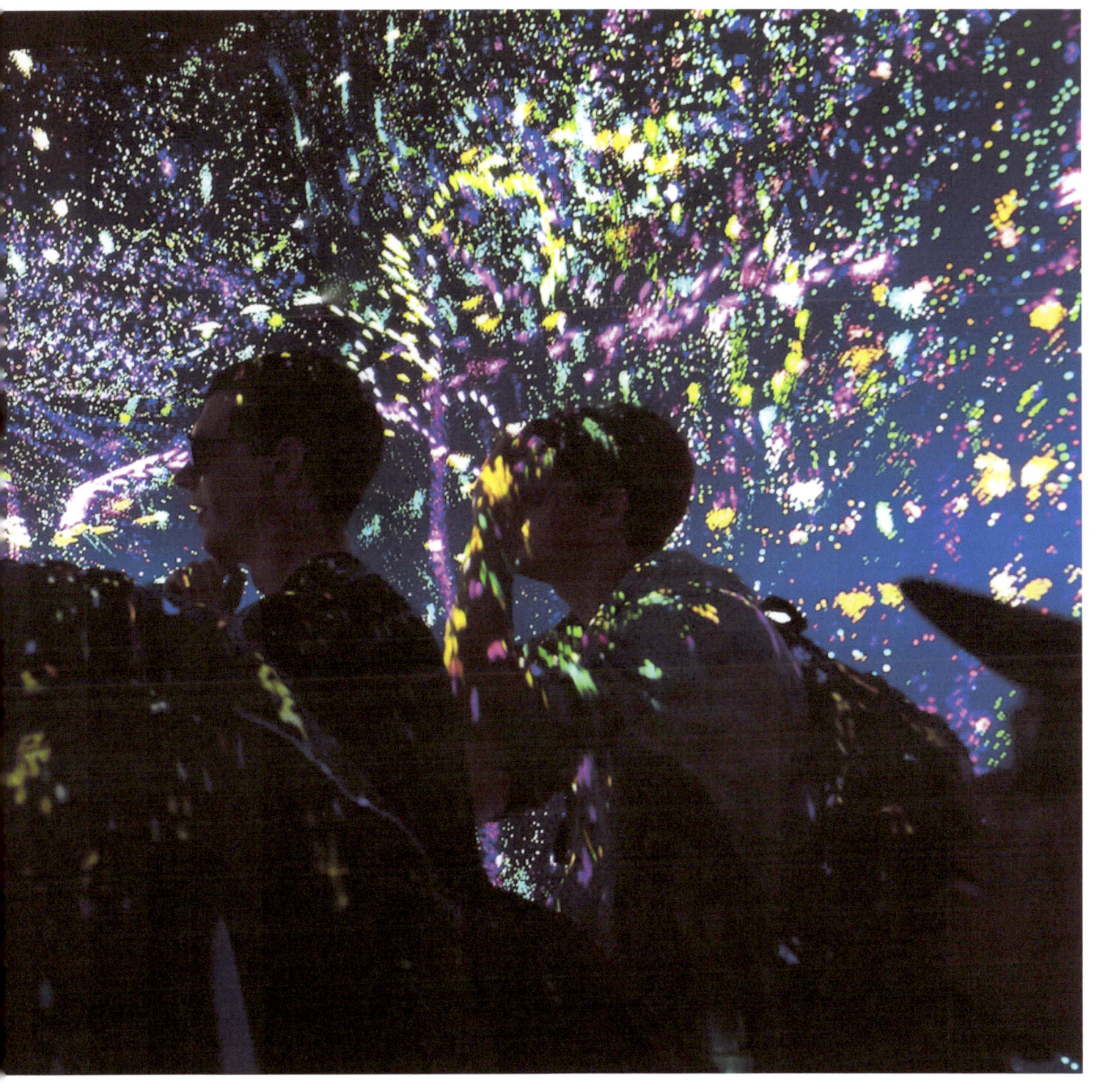

ABOVE: PHOTO OF VIRTUAL-REALITY INSTALLATION, *PARTICLE DREAMS IN SPHERICAL HARMONICS*. PHOTO BY JOHN HANACEK

night in the environs of his lakeside house in Wisconsin, into an almost Blakean meditation on the cosmos that shifts from geological fractals of waterscape to the neural pathways of inner space.

Research aside, Sandin was still very much engaged by an experiential and experimental aesthetic that the film historian P. Adams Sitney described in a book-length study as "visionary." According to Sitney, "the great unacknowledged aspiration of the American avant-garde film has been the cinematic reproduction of the human mind"—an ambition that blended a distinctly Romantic poetics with a McLuhanesque understanding of technology.[11] Sandin, for his part, focused much of his attention on creating an apparatus that could achieve such lofty ends. But as work evolved in the 1980s and the field embraced digital technology, the artist was struck by "how badly matched our tools are to perceptual and effort or systems!"[12] He was critical of the standard computer interface of mouse and keyboard, as well as the narrow angle of the visual field, the poor sound, and the absence of tactile and kinesthetic cues. He continued to work on the DIP and a tool that he called the "People's Video Synthesizer," which would cost $1,000, be as portable as a laptop, and work directly with consumer-grade videotape. He even branched out into computer-generated holography, all in search of that elusive medium that could match the complexity of consciousness and the immediacy and synaesthetic character of perception.

The medium that delivered this experience would come in the early years of the following decade, when Sandin's position at a major research university meant the possibility of working with supercomputers and the availability of capital-intensive resources through National Science Foundation support for data visualization and display. Here Sandin's light-show experience from the mid-1960s served to direct him away from the use of the standard, head-mounted, virtual-reality goggles, and instead toward utilizing projection and an immersive configuration of screens. Equally significant were those distinctive features of video that fueled his first engagement with the medium—interactivity, immediacy, motion—that proved to be key components of the experience.

At UIC Dan Sandin and Tom DeFanti worked side by side in a form of what Sandin dubbed a 'mind meld' to devise a virtual-reality theater. They called it the CAVE Automatic Virtual Environment (CAVE, for short). With its acronym echoing Plato's classical allegory about truth and illusion, the apparatus consisted of an immersive, ten-foot cube with large 3D projections shown on three walls and the floor, across which participants wearing 3D glasses equipped with a tracking device could navigate and interact. Like the IP, the CAVE quickly became a tool for artists and students as well as a paradigm-shifting 21st-century medium capable of realizing the aspirations of earlier generations of artists.

If, as the mythic reading of the field has it, Nam June Paik was the "George Washington of video," then Dan Sandin may well have been its Benjamin Franklin. While Paik, trained in music composition, active in the Fluxus movement, and an acolyte of John Cage, was an artist who worked with electronic technology, Sandin was a scientist-turned-artist who viewed his technological innovations not as art but as instruments for artistic production. As such, Sandin focused much of his career within the practical domain of tool-building, enabling his community to create art with modest, sustainable resources. What has emerged from these efforts over the past four decades is a particularly American form of media—part DIY, part populist form of modernist *détournement* that takes the technologies of the military-entertainment complex and repurposes them for perceptual play, aesthetic experience, and an open-ended mode of cultural communication. Sandin's art works and his instruments will continue to engage new generations of his increasingly global community of artists, students, and colleagues.

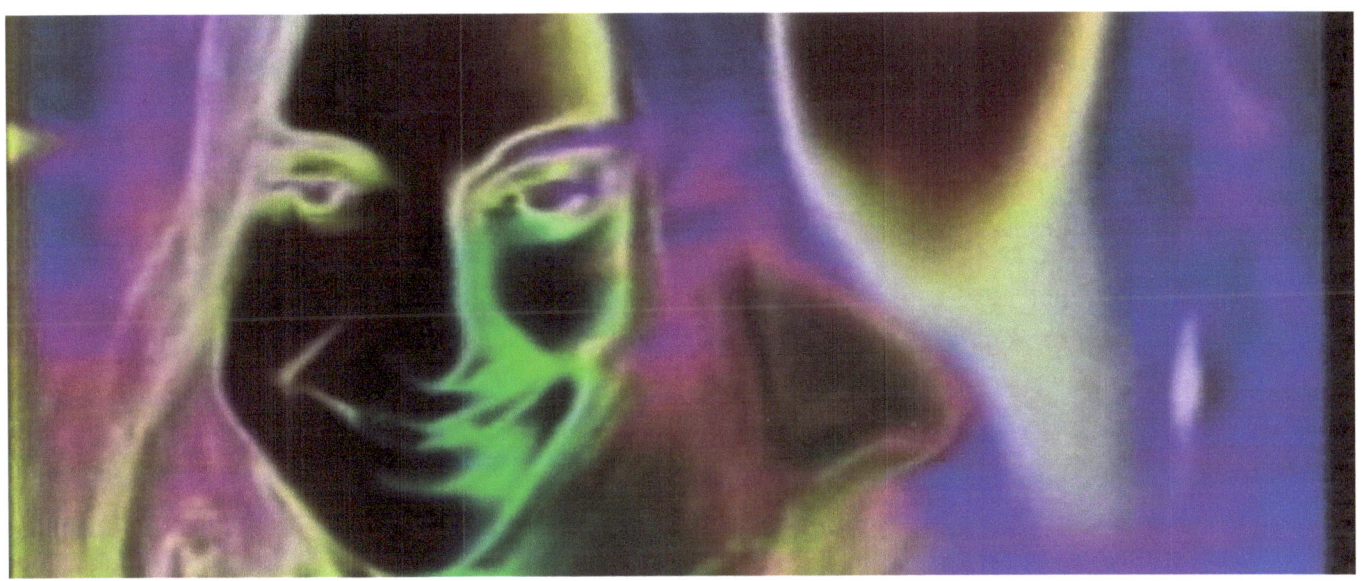

[1] Gene Youngblood quoted in Christine Tamblyn, "Image Processing in Chicago Video Art, 1970–1980," in Leonardo 24, no. 3 (1991): 305.

[2] Gene Youngblood, Expanded Cinema (New York: E. P. Dutton, 1970), 336–37.

[3] Ibid., 318.

[4] Dan Sandin quoted in Lucinda Furlong, "Notes Toward a History of Image-Processed Video," Afterimage 11, nos.
1 & 2 (Summer 1985): 37.

[5] Joyce Bolinger, "Ten Years of the Image Processor—Chicago's Artist/Technologists," Scan 6, no. 3 (Fall 1983): 3.

[6] Tamblyn, "Image Processing in Chicago Video Art," 304.vii Furlong, "Notes Toward a History of Image-Processed Video," 37.

[7] Lucinda Furlong, "Notes Toward a History of Image-Processed Video," 37.

[8] Dan Sandin, "Narrative of Career," typewritten document, c. 1980.

[9] Dan Sandin and Phil Morton, "Distribution Religion," typewritten document, c. 1978, in Furlong, "Notes Toward a History of Image-Processed Video," 38.

[10] Tamblyn, "Image Processing in Chicago Video Art," 305.

[11] P. Adams Sitney, Visionary Film: The American Avant-Garde (New York: Oxford University Press, 1974), 408.

[12] Daniel J. Sandin, "Digital Illusion, Virtual Reality, and Cinema," in Clark Dodsworth, Jr., ed., Digital Illusion: Entertaining the Future with High Technology (New York: ACM Press, 1998), 8.

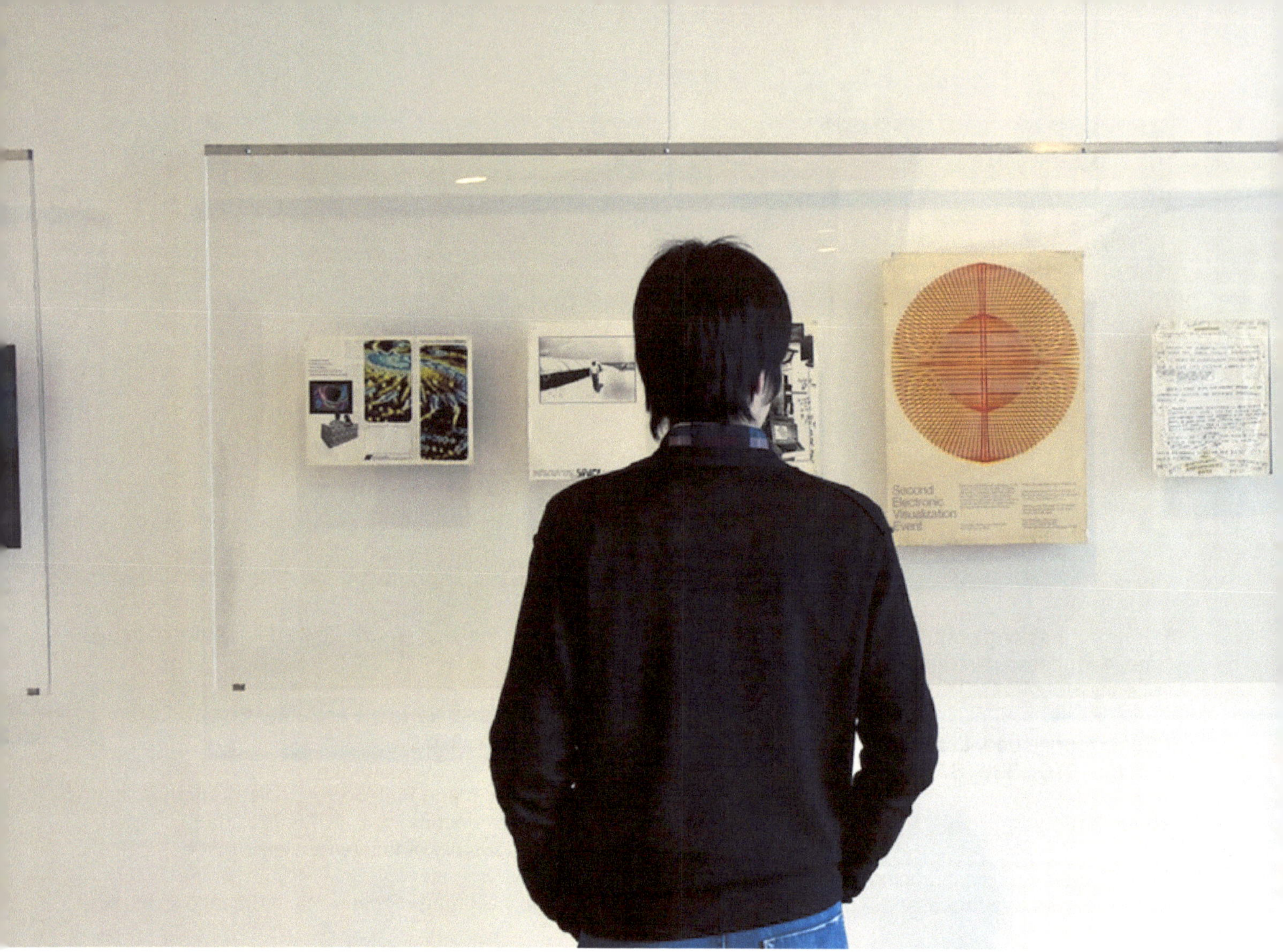

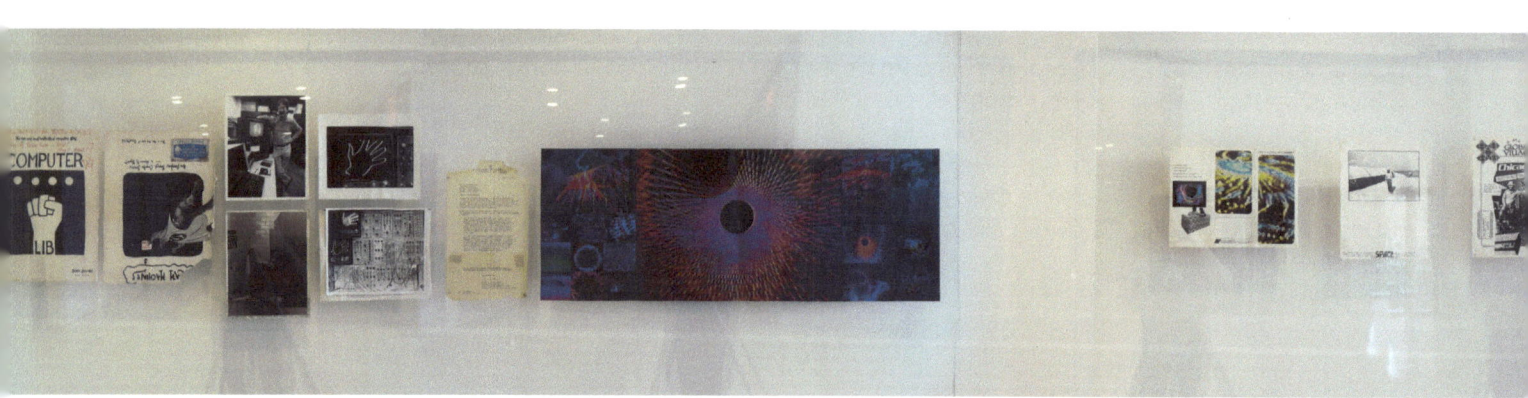

CATALOG N°11
ESSAY BY BRUCE JENKINS

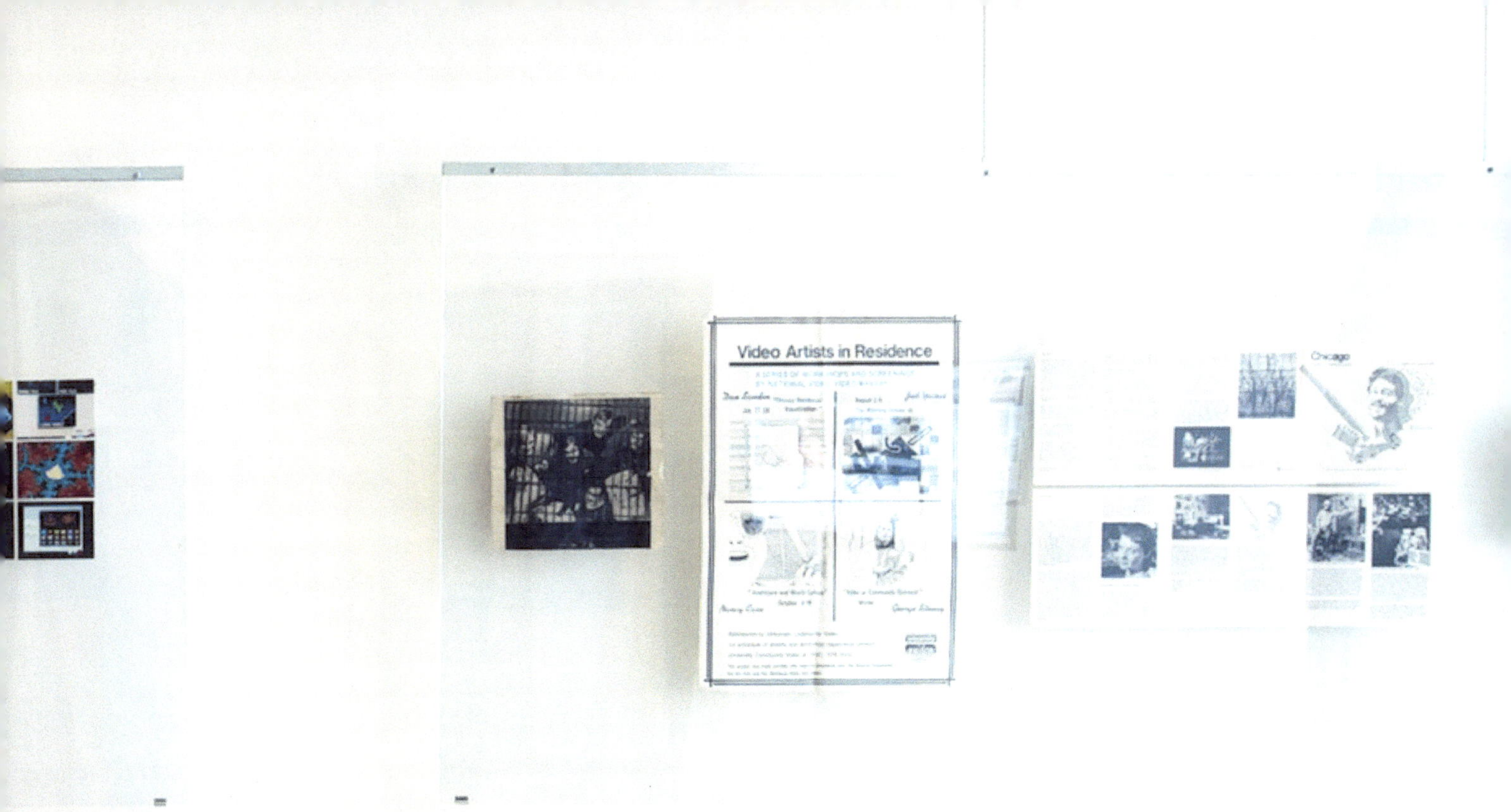

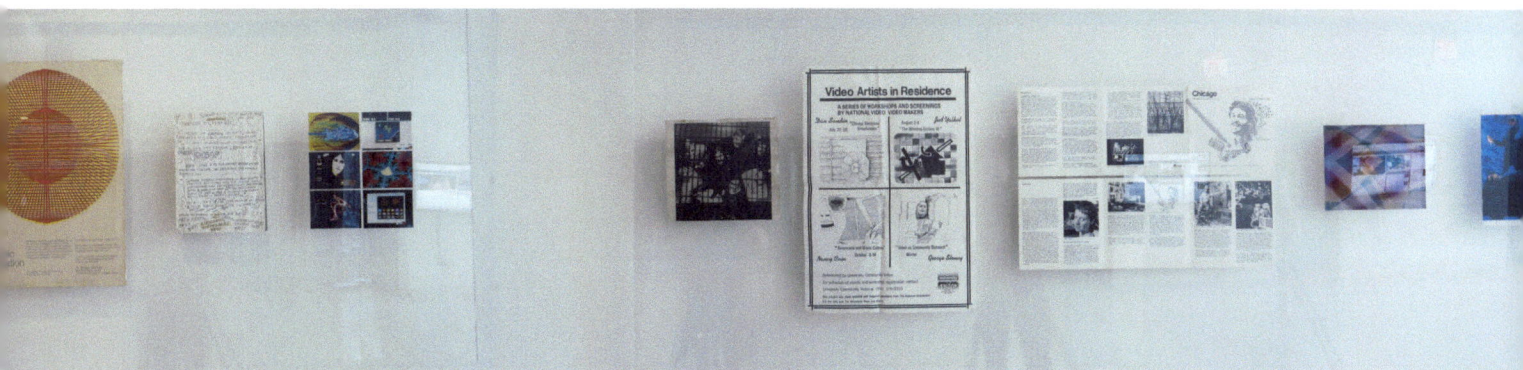

ABOVE: PHOTOS OF THE ENTRANCE AREA OF THE EXHIBITION. PHOTOS BY JOHN HANACEK.

VIDEO GALLERY

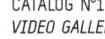

The centerpiece of the "Synthesis: Processing and Collaboration" exhibit in the gallery@calit2 is the wall projection of video art and computer imagery dating back to the very early days of the field. What follows is a brief gallery of titles and still frames from videos by Dan Sandin and colleagues from the early 1970s on, as projected on the main screen and on the four ceiling-mounted displays across from the entrance to the gallery. And furthest below, Sandin's more recent video work displayed in 3D on the Alioscopy autostereo system which offers the ultimate in 21st-century viewing technology – three-dimensional viewing without the need for 3D glasses.

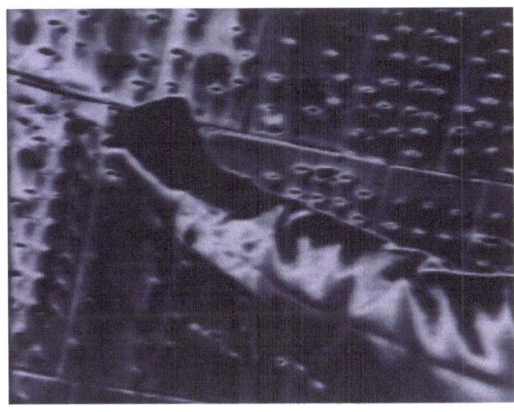

5 minute Romp Through the IP, 1973
–Dan Sandin, Phil Morton

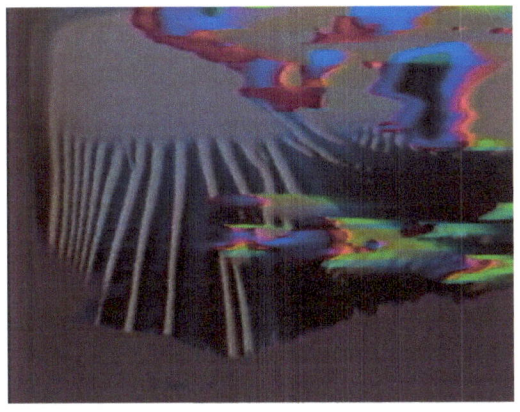

Colorful Colorado, ˜1976
–Phil Morton, Stuart Pettigrew

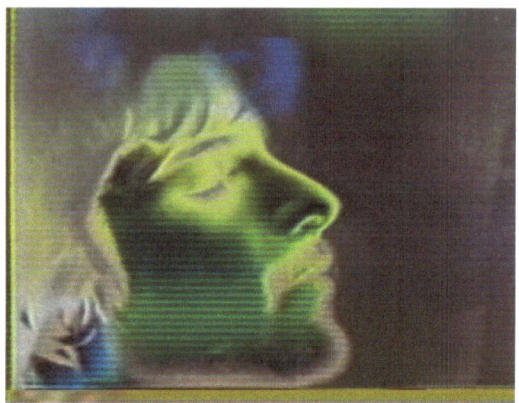

Interactive Installations, 1977 and '78
Speak to Me Softly
–Annette Barbier, Richard Mandeberg
Photo Booth at Center Focus
–Drew Browning, edited by Greg Dawe
The IP was the controlling computer and video image processor.

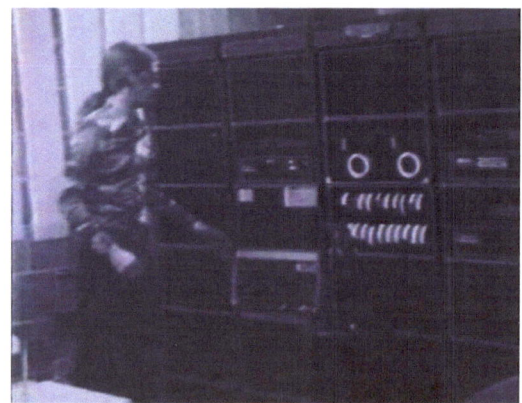

Poop for the National Computer Conference, 1975
–Tom DeFanti, Phil Morton and Dan Sandin

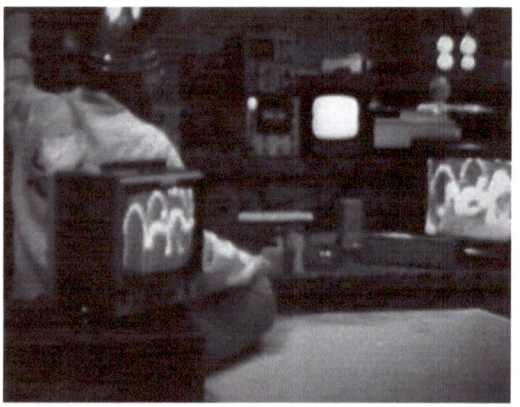

Spiral 1, 1975
–Raul Zaritsky and Jim Morrissette
Document of performance at Electronic Visualization Event 1 in Chicago,
April 1975

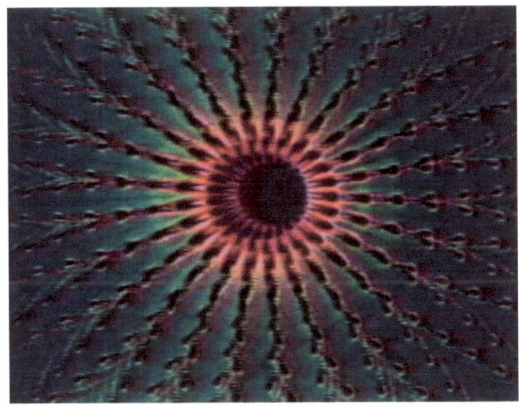

Spiral 5 PTL (Perhaps The Last), 1979
–Dan Sandin, Tom DeFanti and Mimi Shevitz
Live recording of performance before a small studio audience

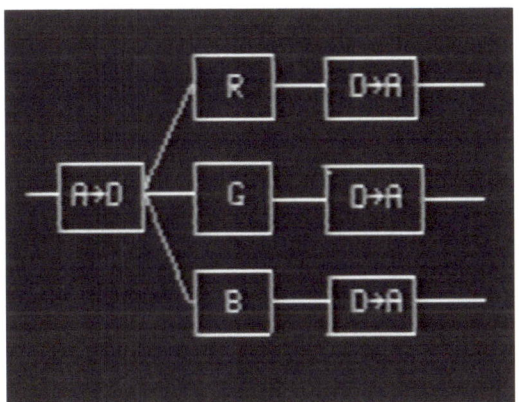

The Digital Image Colorizer, 1979
–Dan Sandin

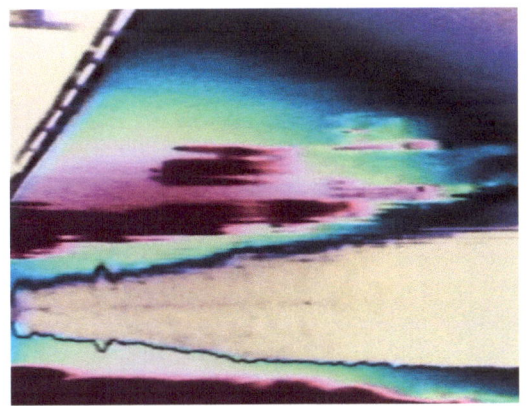

Wandawega Waters, 1979
–Dan Sandin
The Sandin family vacation home on Lake Wandawega, videotaped in one day

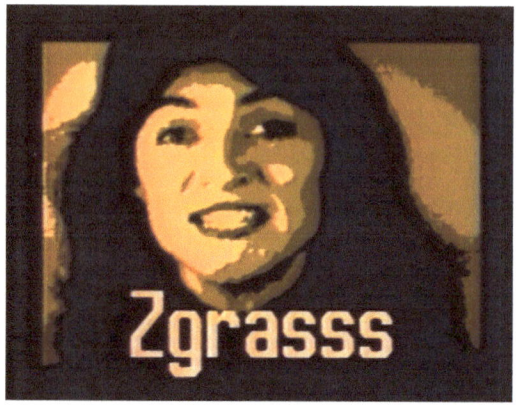

Real-Time Design ZGRASS Demo, 1980
–Jane Veeder, Raul Zaritsky, Copper Giloth
Created with Datamax UV-1 Zgrass Computer

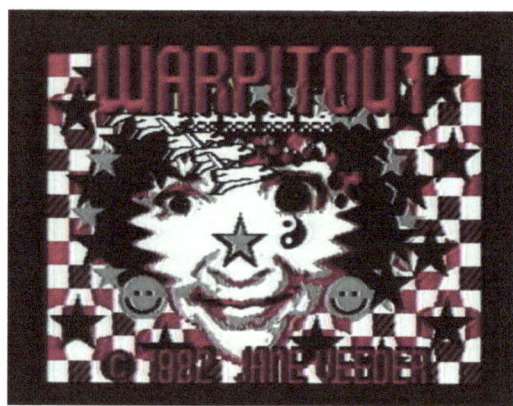

Warpitout, 1982
–Jane Veeder
Created with Datamax UV-1 Zgrass Computer

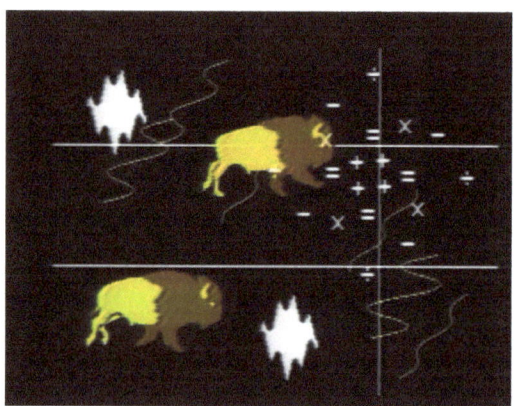

Floater (The Final Sequence), 1982
–Jane Veeder
Created with Datamax UV-1 Zgrass Computer

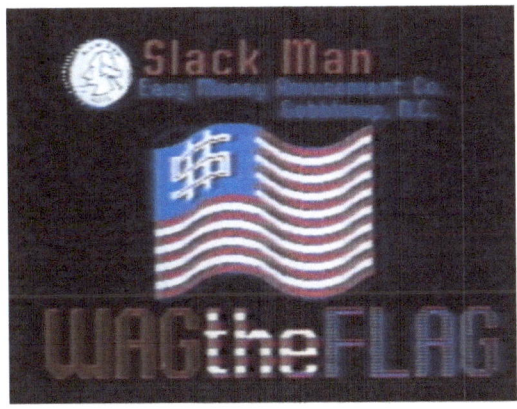

Wag the Flag, 1984
–Charles Kesler and David Balch
–Music by Robert Watson
–Music recording by Richard Royall

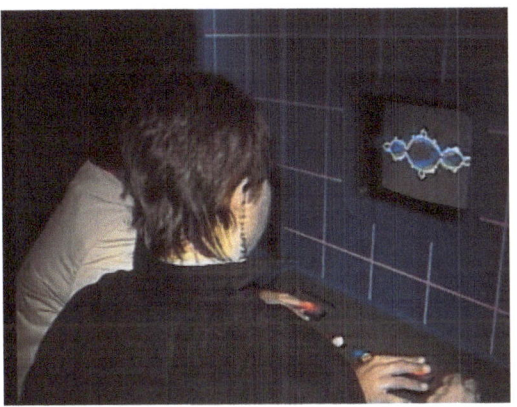

Interactive Image, 1987-88
–Tom DeFanti and everyone from Electronic Visualization Laboratory

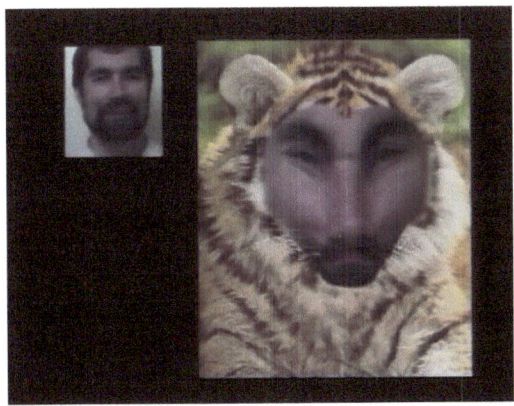

Beauty and the Beast, 1989
–Mary Rassmussen

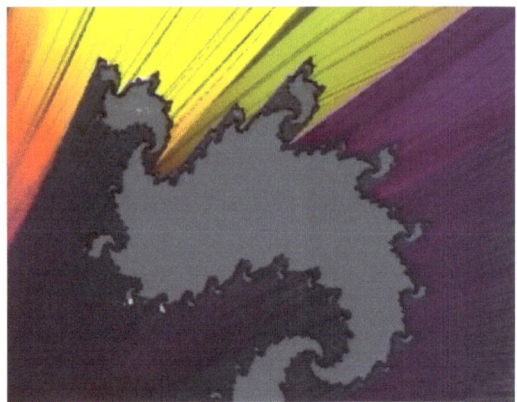

A Volume of 2-Dimensional Julia Sets, ~1990
–Computer graphics and RT/1 programming: Dan Sandin
–Original music and audio effects: Laurie Spiegel
–Algorithms & ray-tracer: John Hart
–Mathematical research: Lou Kauffman
–Visual leadership: Tom DeFanti

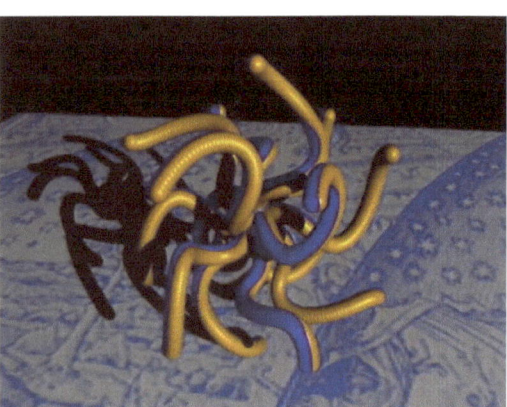

Air on the Dirac Strings, 1993
–Concept: George Francis, Louis Kauffman, Dan Sandin
–Computer graphics: Chris Hartman, John Hart
–Dance: Jan Heyn Cubacub
–Editor: Dana Plepys
–Music: Sumit Das

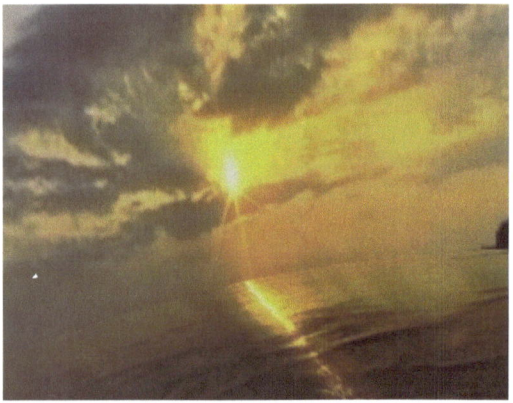

From Death's Door to the Garden Peninsula, 1999
–Virtual environment: Dan Sandin
–Sound: Laurie Spiegel
–Kayaking partner: Dick Ainsworth
–Electronic Visualization partner: Tom DeFanti

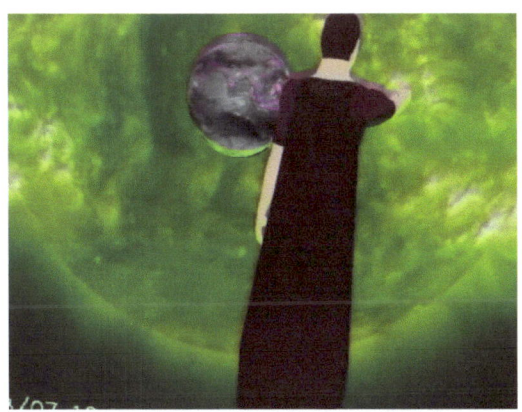

EVL Alive on the Grid, 2001
–Dan Sandin, Josephine Anstey, Geoffrey Allen Baum, Drew Browning, Beth Cerny Patiño, Margaret Dolinsky, Petra Gemeinboeck, Marientina Gotsis, Alex Hill, Ya Lu Lin, Josephine Lipuma, Brenda Lopez Silva, Todd Margolis, Keith Miller, Dave Pape, Tim Portlock, Joseph Tremonti, Annette Barbier, Dan Neveu

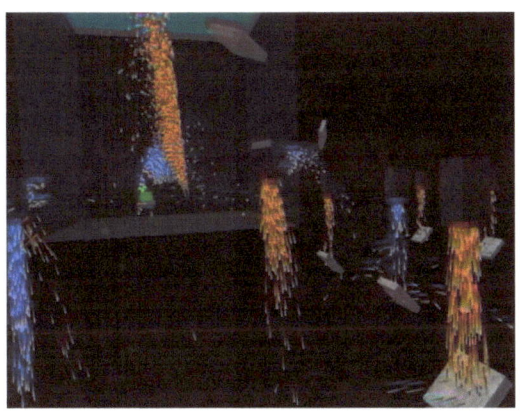

Looking for Water, 2001-2005
–Dan Sandin

Video Playback on LCD Displays

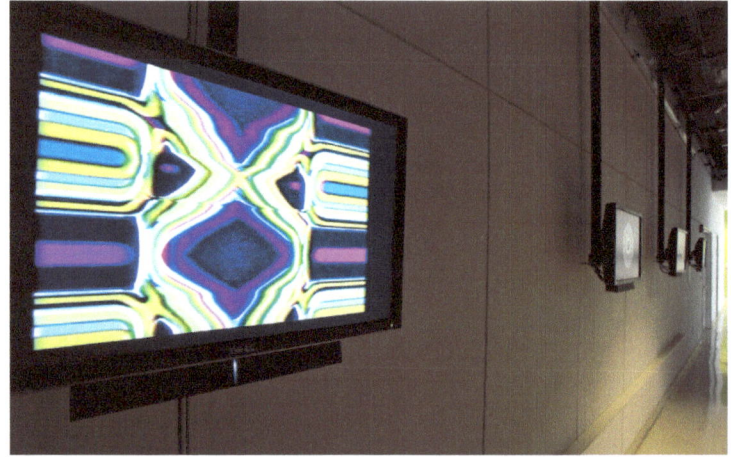

Electronic Visualization Event 3 Distribution Tape,
1978 –First shown in Chicago, IL, May 1978

Wire Trees with 4 Vectors
Audio: Lief Brush, Stu Pettigrew
Video: Phil Morton, Guenther Tetz

By the Crimson Bands of Cyttorak
Audio: Glen Charvat, Doug Lofstrom, Rick Panzer, Jim
Teister
Video: Tom DeFanti, Barbara Sykes

Electronic Masks
Audio: Glen Charvat, Doug Lofstrom, Tom Warzecha
Video: Barbara Sykes

Spiral3
Audio: Sticks Raboin, Bob Snyder
Video: Tom DeFanti, Phil Morton, Dan Sandin, Jane
Veeder
Dance: Rylin Harris

Digital TV Dinner
Audio: Dick Ainsworth
Video: Jay Fenton, Raul Zaritsky

Data Bursts in 3 Moves
Audio Phil Morton, Bob Snyder
Video Phil Morton, Guenther Tetz

Cetacean
Audio: Barry Brosch, Chip Dodsworth
Video: Chip Dodsworth, Phil Morton

Not of This Earth
Audio: Patti Smith
Video: Barbra Latham, John Manning, Ed Rankus

Video Playback on Alioscopy Autostereo Display

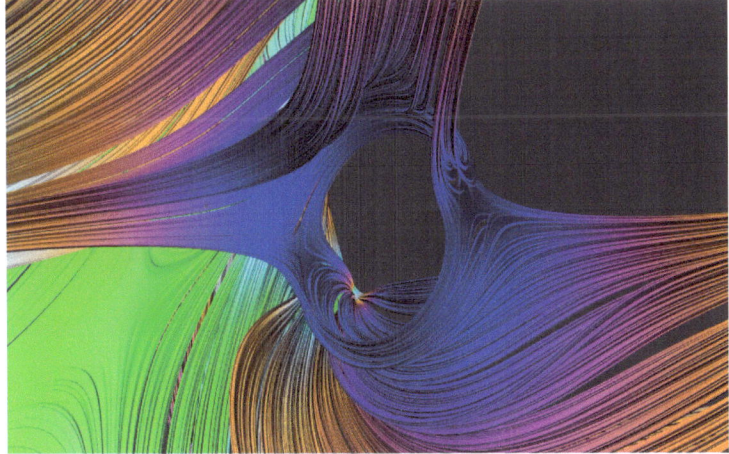

A Study of 4D Julia Sets: Iterations of Z = Z2 +K in the Quaternions, 2005 by Dan Sandin

–Animation: Dan Sandin
–Algorithms: John Hart, Yumei Dang
–Programming: Dan Sandin, Shalini Venkataraman
–Visionary Leadership: Tom DeFanti
–Mathematical leadership: Louis Kauffman
–Music Composition and Performance: Stephan Vankov

(Produced at the Electronic Visualization Laboratory, UIC, and Calit2, UCSD)

PARTICLE DREAMS

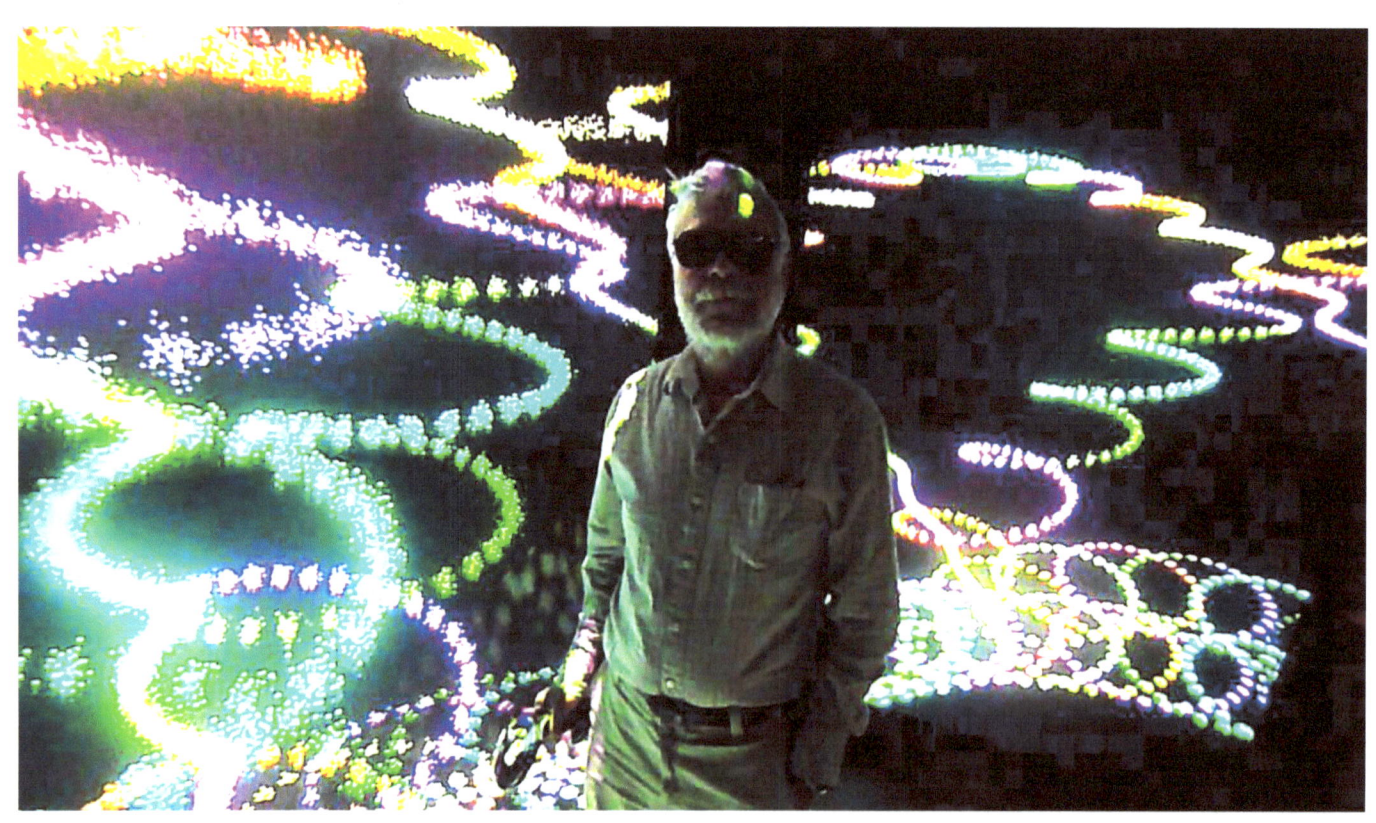

The virtual-reality installation, Particle Dreams in Spherical Harmonics, created for this show, is the latest of a series of VR art installations created by Dan Sandin and collaborators to involve the viewer-participant in the creation of an immersive, visual and sonic experience. It is based on the physical simulation of over one million particles with momentum and elastic reflection in an environment with gravity. In the final scene there is a very realistic rendering of water with reflections, and lighting based on spherical harmonics. The sound components are triggered and modified by the user and particle interaction.

The subjective experience of Particle Dreams in Calit2's StarCAVE 360-degree, 3D VR environment is described here by a visitor. According to Amos Jessup, standing in the StarCAVE "was like standing in a rainstorm made of rainbow fragments, with the power to guide the storm by hand. It was unsettling, out-of-body, very trippy stuff, a powerful artistic experience. The sounds, in small fragments like the rainbows, seemed to be natural concomitants of the gestures, even though you could tell it was not through a mechanical linkage, a theremin or one of its descendants. But whatever the linkage was it managed to be sensitive, or else it was just inherent in the genius of the sounds that they seemed that way."

Particle Dreams in Spherical Harmonics
Content and application programming: Dan Sandin
Content and systems programming: Robert Kooima
Music and sound effects: Laurie Spiegel
Driver: Tom DeFanti

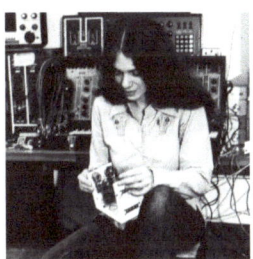

Laurie Spiegel, composer, software creator and visual artist, is known widely for her pioneering work with many early analog and digital electronic music systems, including the GROOVE system at Bell Telephone Labs, and Music Mouse, a software-based musical instrument for Macintosh, Atari and Amiga. Her realization of Kepler's "Harmony of the Planets" was included on the Voyager Spacecraft's "Sounds of Earth" gold record. Often praised for her integration of intellect and intuition, she has taught at Cooper Union and NYU. Spiegel currently lives and works in a large, semi-raw loft in lower Manhattan and in cyberspace.

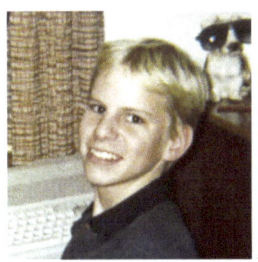

Robert Kooima began collaborating with Sandin and DeFanti while a doctoral student at EVL between 2004 and 2008. He is currently an adjunct professor in the Department of Computer Science at Louisiana State University (LSU), and a post-doctoral researcher with the Arts, Visualization, Advanced Technologies and Research (AVATAR) Initiative at LSU's Center for Computation and Technology. Kooima's work, research and teaching focus on interactive 3D computer graphics, scientific visualization, game development, and stereographic display technology.

Note: Bios for Dan Sandin and Tom DeFanti can be viewed in the Artist Biographies chapter of this catalog.

ARTIST BIOGRAPHY

DANIEL A. SANDIN

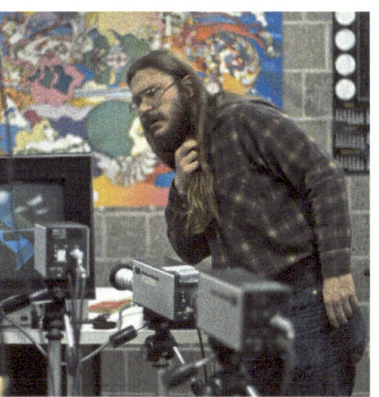

Daniel J. Sandin is an internationally recognized pioneer of electronic art and visualization. He is director emeritus of the Electronic Visualization Lab and a professor emeritus in the School of Art and Design at the University of Illinois at Chicago. He is continuing his professional activities with Tom DeFanti at Calit2, UCSD. As an artist, he has exhibited worldwide, and has received grants in support of his work from the Rockefeller Foundation, the Guggenheim Foundation, the National Science Foundation and the National Endowment for the Arts. His video animation *Spiral PTL* is in the inaugural collection of video art at the Museum of Modern Art in New York.

In 1969, Sandin developed a computer-controlled light and sound environment, called Glow Flow, at the Smithsonian Institution and was invited to join the art faculty at the University of Illinois the same year. By 1973 he had developed the Sandin Image Processor, a highly programmable analog computer for processing video images in real time. He then worked with DeFanti to combine the Image Processor with real-time computer graphics and performed visual concerts, the Electronic Visualization Events, with synthesized musical accompaniment. In 1991, Sandin and DeFanti conceived and developed, in collaboration with graduate students, the CAVE virtual-reality (VR) theater.

In recent years, Sandin has been concentrating on the development of auto stereo VR displays (i.e., free viewing, no glasses), and on the creation of network-based tele-collaborative VR art works that involve video camera image materials, rich human interaction and mathematical systems.

Read more at: http://www.evl.uic.edu/dan/

ARTIST BIOGRAPHY

THOMAS A. DEFANTI

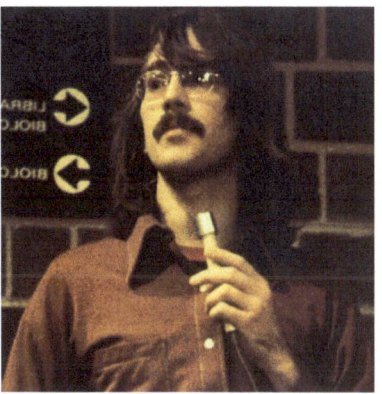

Tom DeFanti, Ph.D., is a Senior Research Scientist in the California Institute for Telecommunications and Information Technology (Calit2) at the University of California, San Diego. He is also a Distinguished Professor Emeritus in Computer Science at the University of Illinois at Chicago (UIC).

DeFanti is Principal Investigator (PI) of the NSF International Research Network Connections Program TransLight/StarLight project; PI of the KAUST Calit2 OptIPresence project; and PI of the NSF-funded GreenLight Instrument project. GreenLight uses optical networks to connect scientists and their labs to more energy-efficient 'green' computer processing and storage systems.

DeFanti is an internationally recognized expert in computer graphics since the early 1970s. He has amassed a number of credits, including: use of his lab's hardware and software for the computer animation sequence produced for the 1977 *Star Wars* movie; recipient of the 1988 ACM Outstanding Contribution Award; and appointed an ACM Fellow in 1994. He also shares recognition, with EVL director Daniel J. Sandin, for conceiving the CAVE virtual-reality theater in 1991.

Striving for more than a decade to connect high-resolution visualization and virtual-reality devices over long distances, DeFanti has collaborated with Larry Smarr, Maxine Brown, Joe Mambretti, Tomonori Aoyama, and Kees Neggers to lead state, national and international teams to build the most advanced, production-quality networks available to scientists, with major NSF funding. He is a founding member of the Global Lambda Integrated Facility (GLIF), a group that manages international, switched-wavelength networks for research and education. In the United States, DeFanti established the 10 Gigabit Ethernet CAVEwave research network—a model for future, high-end science and engineering collaboration infrastructure. The CAVEwave linked EVL and StarLight in Chicago to the Pacific Northwest GigaPop in Seattle, and UCSD/Calit2 in San Diego, in support of CineGrid, OptIPlatform and other national/international research uses.

ACKNOWLEDGMENTS

An exhibition such as "Synthesis: Processing and Collaboration," which looks back to Chicago video art from the 1970s in order to inform current practice in virtual reality, requires a bit of time travel on the part of the artists, researchers and staff who contributed to the show. I would like to thank Dan Sandin and Tom DeFanti for their willingness to dig into their personal archives, to unearth a history that makes visible the unique relationships between EVL and Calit2, Chicago and San Diego, and art and science. The resulting exhibition provides an educational experience for both seasoned staff at Calit2 and students at UCSD who may be exposed to this work for the first time. Sandin and DeFanti would like to extend "Four decades of thanks to our enlightened UIC leaders, and all the EVL faculty, staff, and students. 25 years of thanks to Larry Smarr. And a decade of thanks to everyone at Calit2, UCSD Division."

In particular, acknowledgments are due to Sheldon Brown, Director of the Center for Research in Computing and the Arts, for proposing the exhibition and seeing it through to completion, along with the support of the Gallery Committee and Ramesh Rao, Director of Calit2's UCSD Division. The Calit2 A/V team, led by Hector Bracho, and including Mike Toillion, Emily Jankowski, Quan Le and Laura Park, was indispensable as always in the installation and formatting (from Betacam!) of videos for the exhibition. Gallery Assistants Christina Telya, Joey Ma, Tony Lu, Vanessa Neag, Andrew Wang, and Christina Eco helped install the exhibition and opened it for visitors throughout the show. Special thanks are due to Greg Dawe and Todd Margolis, for their generosity and guidance. The virtual-reality piece "Particle Dreams" could not have been completed without the talent and expertise of Robert Kooima and Laurie Spiegel. We are all extremely grateful to Joe Reitzer, for saving from the trash, storing for 20 years and resurrecting the Sandin Image Processors numbers 1, 3 and 4, without which the Image Processor installation would not have been possible. Thanks, too, go to Ken Rehor for use of his photograph of the "Inflatable TV". Finally, thanks go to the Calit2 Communications team, under the direction of Doug Ramsey, and including Cristian Horta, Alex Matthews, Tiffany Fox and John Hanacek, who photographed, recorded, wrote, and did the layout for this publication.

-Trish Stone, Gallery Coordinator

gallery@calit2 reflects the nexus of innovation implicit in Calit2's vision, and aims to advance our understanding and appreciation of the dynamic interplay among art, science and technology.

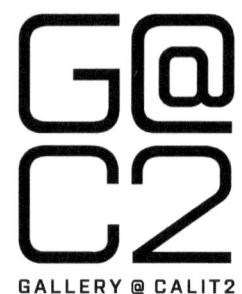

GALLERY @ CALIT2

First Floor
Atkinson Hall
9500 Gilman Drive
University of California, San Diego
La Jolla, CA 92093

http://gallery.calit2.net

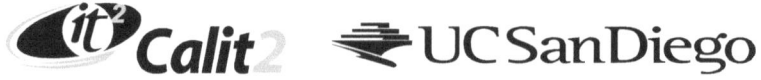

www.ingramcontent.com/pod-product-compliance
Lightning Source LLC
Chambersburg PA
CBHW051055180526
45172CB00002B/646